New Arduino Communication Projects using MATLAB and Sensors

Copyright © Anbazhagan.k

New Arduino Communication Projects using MATLAB and Sensors

CONTENTS

Acknowledgments 5

Introduction 6

1.How to use SPI in Arduino: Communication 7
between two Arduino Boards

2.Build a Smart Watch by Interfacing OLED 32
Display with Android Phone using Arduino

3.DIY Waveform Generator using Arduino 56

4.How to use Bluetooth with MATLAB for 79
Wireless Communication

5.How to Burn Arduino Bootloader in 97
Atemga328 IC and Program it using Arduino IDE

6.Thermal Printer Interfacing with Arduino 115
Uno

7.Digital Compass using Arduino and 130
HMC5883L Magnetometer

8.How to Plot Real Time Temperature Graph 154
using MATLAB

9.Serial Communication between MATLAB 171

and Arduino

10.Stepper Motor Control using MATLAB and   189
Arduino

ACKNOWLEDGMENTS

The writer might want to recognize the diligent work of the article group in assembling this book. He might likewise want to recognize the diligent work of the Raspberry Pi Foundation and the Arduino bunch for assembling items and networks that help to make the Internet Of Things increasingly open to the overall population. Yahoo for the democratization of innovation!

INTRODUCTION

The Internet of Things (IOT) is a perplexing idea comprised of numerous PCs and numerous correspondence ways. Some IOT gadgets are associated with the Internet and some are most certainly not. Some IOT gadgets structure swarms that convey among themselves. Some are intended for a solitary reason, while some are increasingly universally useful PCs. This book is intended to demonstrate to you the IOT from the back to front. By structure IOT gadgets, the per user will comprehend the essential ideas and will almost certainly develop utilizing the rudiments to make his or her very own IOT applications. These included ventures will tell the per user the best way to assemble their very own IOT ventures and to develop the models appeared. The significance of Computer Security in IOT gadgets is additionally talked about and different systems for protecting the IOT from unapproved clients or programmers. The most significant takeaway from this book is in structure the tasks yourself.

1.HOW TO USE SPI IN ARDUINO: COMMUNICATION BETWEEN TWO ARDUINO BOARDS

A Microcontroller utilizes a large range of conventions to speak with different sensors and peripherals. There are numerous conventions for remote and wired correspondence, and the most ordinarily utilized correspondence method is Serial Communication. Sequential correspondence is the way toward sending information one piece at once, consecutively, over a correspondence channel or transport. There are numerous kinds of sequential correspondence like UART, CAN, USB, I2C and SPI correspondence.

In this instructional exercise we find out about SPI convention and how to utilize it in Arduino. We will utilize SPI Protocol for correspondence between two Arduinos. Here one Arduino will go about as Master as well as another will go about as Slave, two LEDs and push catches will be associated with both the arduinos. To exhibit SPI correspondence, we will control ace side LED by the push catch at slave side and the other way around utilizing the SPI Serial correspondence convention.

What is SPI?

SPI (Serial Peripheral Interface) is a sequential correspondence convention. SPI interface was found by Motorola in 1970. SPI has a full duplex association, which implies that the information is sent as well as got at the mean time. That is an ace can send information to slave and a slave can send information to ace at the mean time. SPI is synchronous sequential correspondence implies the clock is required for correspondence reason.

SPI correspondence is recently clarified in different microcontrollers:

1. SPI Communication with PIC Microcontroller PIC16F877A

2. Interfacing 3.5 inch contact screen tft lcd with raspberry pi

3. programming avr microcontroller with spi pins

4. interfacing nokia 5110 graphical lcd with arduino

Working of SPI

A SPI has an ace/Slave correspondence by utilizing four lines. A SPI can have just one ace and can have different slaves. An ace is normally a microcontroller and the slaves can be a microcontroller, sensors, ADC, DAC, LCD and so on.

The following is the square graph portrayal of SPI Master with Single Slave.

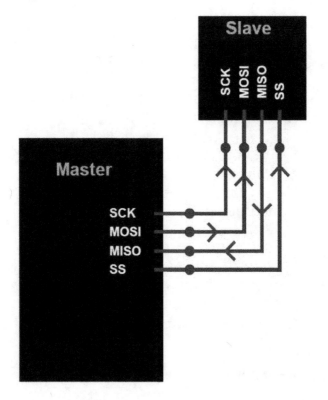

SPI has following four lines MISO, MOSI, SS, and CLK

1. MISO (Master in Slave Out) - The Slave line for sending information to the ace.

2. MOSI (Master Out Slave In) - The Master line for sending information to the peripherals.

3. SCK (Serial Clock) - The clock beats which synchronize information transmission created by the ace.

4. SS (Slave Select) - Master can utilize this stick to empower and cripple explicit gadgets.

SPI Master with Multiple Slaves

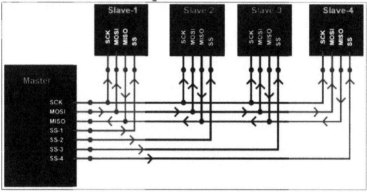

To begin correspondence among ace and slave we have to set the required gadget's Slave Select (SS) stick to LOW, so it can speak with the ace. At the point when it's high, it disregards the ace. This enables you to have different SPI gadgets having a similar MISO, MOSI, and CLK lines of ace. As should be obvious in the above picture there are four slaves in which the SCLK, MISO, MOSI are basic associated with ace and the SS of each slave is associated independently to singular SS pins (SS1, SS2, SS3) of ace. By setting the required SS stick LOW an ace can speak with that slave.

SPI Pins in Arduino UNO

The picture beneath demonstrates the SPI pins present Arduino UNO (in red box).

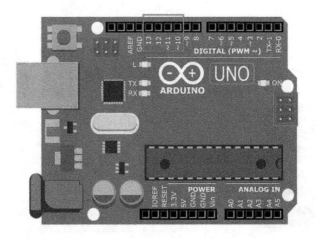

SPI Line	Pin in Arduino
MOSI	11 or ICSP-4
MISO	12 or ICSP-1
SCK	13 or ICSP-3
SS	10

Using SPI in Arduino

Before begin programming for SPI correspondence between two Arduinos. We have to find out about the SPI library utilized in Arduino IDE.

The library <SPI.h> is incorporated into the program for utilizing the accompanying capacities for SPI correspondence.

1. SPI.begin()

USE: To Initialize the SPI transport by setting SCK, MOSI, as well as SS to yields, pulling SCK as well as MOSI low, as well as SS high.

2. SPI.setClockDivider(divider)

USE: To Set the SPI clock divider with respect to the framework clock. The accessible dividers are 2, 4, 8, 16, 32, 64 or 128.

Dividers:

- SPI_CLOCK_DIV2

- SPI_CLOCK_DIV4

- SPI_CLOCK_DIV8

- SPI_CLOCK_DIV16

- SPI_CLOCK_DIV32

- SPI_CLOCK_DIV64

- SPI_CLOCK_DIV128

3. SPI.attachInterrupt(handler)

USE: This capacity is considered when a slave gadget gets information from the ace.

4. SPI.transfer(val)

USE: This capacity is utilized to concurrent send and get the information among ace and slave.

So now how about we begin with down to earth show of SPI convention in Arduino. In this instructional exercise we will utilize two arduino one as ace and different as slave. Both Arduino are connected with a LED and a push catch independently. Ace LED can be constrained by utilizing slave Arduino's push catch and slave Arduino's LED can be constrained by ace Arduino's push catch utilizing SPI correspondence convention present in arduino.

Components Required

- Resistor 2.2k (2)
- LED (2)
- Arduino UNO (2)
- Push Button (2)
- Resistor 10k (2)
- Connecting Wires
- Breadboard

Arduino SPI Communication Circuit Diagram

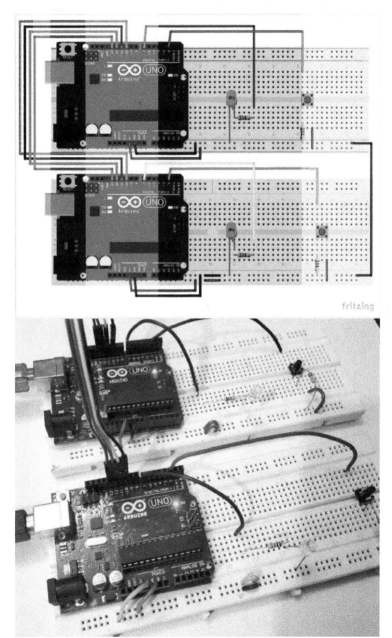

Programming Explanation

This instructional exercise has two projects one for ace arduino as well as other for slave arduino. Complete projects for both the sides are given toward the part of the arrangement.

Master Arduino Programming Explanation

1. Above all else we have to incorporate the SPI library for utilizing SPI correspondence capacities.

```
#include<SPI.h>
```

2. In void arrangement()

- We Start Serial Communication at Baud Rate 115200.

```
Serial.begin(115200);
```

- Join LED to stick 7 and Push catch to stick 2 and set those pins OUTPUT and INPUT individually.

```
pinMode(ipbutton,INPUT);

pinMode(LED,OUTPUT);
```

- Next we start the SPI correspondence

SPI.begin();

- Next we set the Clockdivider for SPI correspondence. Here we have set divider 8.

SPI.setClockDivider(SPI_CLOCK_DIV8);

- At that point set the SS stick HIGH since we didn't begin any exchange to slave arduino.

---

digitalWrite(SS,HIGH);

---

3. In void circle():

- We read the status of the pushbutton stick associated with pin2 (Master Arduino) for sending those incentive to the slave Arduino.

---

buttonvalue = digitalRead(ipbutton);

- Set Logic for Setting x esteem (To be sent to slave) contingent on contribution from stick 2

```
if(buttonvalue == HIGH)

{

  x = 1;

}

else

{

  x = 0;

}
```

- Before sending the worth we have to LOW the slave select an incentive to start move to slave from ace.

```
digitalWrite(SS, LOW);
```

- Here comes the significant advance, in the accompanying explanation we send the push catch worth put away in Mastersend variable to the slave arduino and furthermore get an incentive from slave that will be store in

Mastereceive variable.

```
Mastereceive=SPI.transfer(Mastersend);
```

- After that relying on the Mastereceive esteem we will turn the Master Arduino LED
ON or OFF.

```
if(Mastereceive == 1)

{

  digitalWrite(LED,HIGH);    //Sets pin 7 HIGH

  Serial.println("Master LED ON");

}

else

{

  digitalWrite(LED,LOW);    //Sets pin 7 LOW

  Serial.println("Master LED OFF");

}
```

Note: We use serial.println() to see the outcome in Serial Motor of Arduino IDE.

Slave Arduino Programming Explanation

1. As a matter of first importance we have to incorporate the SPI library for utilizing SPI correspondence capacities.

```
#include<SPI.h>
```

2. In void arrangement()

- We Start Serial Communication at Baud Rate 115200.

```
Serial.begin(115200);
```

- Append LED to stick 7 and Push catch to pin2 and set those pins OUTPUT and INPUT separately.

```
pinMode(ipbutton,INPUT);

pinMode(LED,OUTPUT);
```

- The significant advance here is the accompanying proclamations

```
pinMode(MISO,OUTPUT);
```

The above proclamation sets MISO as OUTPUT (Have to Send information to Master IN). So information is sent through MISO of Slave Arduino.

- Presently Turn on SPI in Slave Mode by utilizing SPI Control Register

```
SPCR |= _BV(SPE);
```

- At that point turn ON hinder for SPI correspondence. On the off chance that an information is gotten from ace the Interrupt Routine is called and the got worth is taken from SPDR (SPI information Register)

```
SPI.attachInterrupt();
```

- The incentive from ace is taken from SPDR and put away in Slavereceived variable. This happens in following Interrupt Routine capacity.

```
ISR (SPI_STC_vect)
```

```
{

  Slavereceived = SPDR;

  received = true;

}
```

3. Next in void circle () we set the Slave arduino LED to turn ON or OFF contingent on the Slavereceived esteem.

```
if (Slavereceived==1)

  {

  digitalWrite(LEDpin,HIGH); //Sets pin 7 as
HIGH LED ON

                       Serial.println("Slave     LED
ON");

  }

else

  {

  digitalWrite(LEDpin,LOW); //Sets pin 7 as LOW
```

LED OFF

Serial.println("Slave LED OFF");

   }

- Next we read the status of the Slave Arduino Push catch and store the incentive in Slavesend to send the incentive to Master Arduino by offering an incentive to SPDR register.

```
buttonvalue = digitalRead(buttonpin);

 if(buttonvalue == HIGH)

    {

      x=1;

    }

else

    {

      x=0;
```

```
    }

        Slavesend=x;

        SPDR = Slavesend;
```

Note: We use serial.println() to see the outcome in Serial Motor of Arduino IDE.

Testing the hardware

The following is the image of conclusive arrangement for SPI correspondence between two Arduino Boards.

At the point when push catch at Master side is squeezed, white LED at slave side turns ON.

Furthermore, when push catch at Slave side is squeezed, Red LED at Master side turns ON.

Anbazhagan k

The total code for Master and Slave Arduino is given underneath.

Code

Master Arduino Code:
```
//SPI MASTER (ARDUINO)
//SPI COMMUNICATION BETWEEN TWO ARDUINO

#include<SPI.h>              //Library for SPI
#define LED 7
#define ipbutton 2
int buttonvalue;
int x;
void setup (void)
```

```
{
 Serial.begin(115200);          //Starts Serial Commu-
nication at Baud Rate 115200


  pinMode(ipbutton,INPUT);              //Sets pin 2 as
input
 pinMode(LED,OUTPUT);          //Sets pin 7 as Output


  SPI.begin();              //Begins the SPI commnuica-
tion
   SPI.setClockDivider(SPI_CLOCK_DIV8);        //Sets
clock for SPI communication at 8 (16/8=2Mhz)
 digitalWrite(SS,HIGH);            // Setting SlaveSelect
as HIGH (So master doesnt connnect with slave)
}
void loop(void)
{
 byte Mastersend,Mastereceive;
  buttonvalue = digitalRead(ipbutton);   //Reads the
status of the pin 2
 if(buttonvalue == HIGH)          //Logic for Setting x
value (To be sent to slave) depending upon input from
pin 2
 {
  x = 1;
 }
 else
 {
  x = 0;
```

```
}


  digitalWrite(SS, LOW);          //Starts communica-
tion with Slave connected to master


  Mastersend = x;
  Mastereceive=SPI.transfer(Mastersend); //Send the
mastersend value to slave also receives value from
slave


  if(Mastereceive == 1)             //Logic for setting
the LED output depending upon value received from
slave
  {
  digitalWrite(LED,HIGH);        //Sets pin 7 HIGH
  Serial.println("Master LED ON");
  }
  else
  {
  digitalWrite(LED,LOW);         //Sets pin 7 LOW
  Serial.println("Master LED OFF");
  }
  delay(1000);
}
```

Slave Arduino Code:
```
//SPI SLAVE (ARDUINO)
//SPI COMMUNICATION BETWEEN TWO ARDUINO
```

```
#include<SPI.h>
#define LEDpin 7
#define buttonpin 2
volatile boolean received;
volatile byte Slavereceived,Slavesend;
int buttonvalue;
int x;
void setup()
{
 Serial.begin(115200);


 pinMode(buttonpin,INPUT);      // Setting pin 2 as
INPUT
 pinMode(LEDpin,OUTPUT);          // Setting pin 7 as
OUTPUT
 pinMode(MISO,OUTPUT);        //Sets MISO as OUT-
PUT (Have to Send data to Master IN
 SPCR |= _BV(SPE);        //Turn on SPI in Slave Mode
 received = false;
 SPI.attachInterrupt();     //Interuupt ON is set for
SPI commnucation


}
ISR (SPI_STC_vect)              //Inerrrput routine
function
{
  Slavereceived = SPDR;       // Value received from
master if store in variable slavereceived
```

```
 received = true;            //Sets received as True
}
void loop()
{ if(received)              //Logic to SET LED ON OR OFF
depending upon the value recerived from master
  {
  if(Slavereceived==1)
  {
  digitalWrite(LEDpin,HIGH);    //Sets pin 7 as HIGH
LED ON
   Serial.println("Slave LED ON");
  }else
  {
  digitalWrite(LEDpin,LOW);    //Sets pin 7 as LOW
LED OFF
   Serial.println("Slave LED OFF");
  }


    buttonvalue = digitalRead(buttonpin);  // Reads
the status of the pin 2


    if(buttonvalue == HIGH)            //Logic to set the
value of x to send to master
  {
  x=1;

    }else
  {
```

```
  x=0;
 }


 Slavesend=x;
 SPDR = Slavesend;              //Sends the x value to
master via SPDR
 delay(1000);
}
}
```

2.BUILD A SMART WATCH BY INTERFACING OLED DISPLAY WITH ANDROID PHONE USING ARDUINO

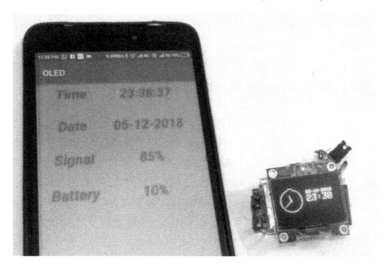

A huge portion of us would be comfortable with the 16×2 Dot grid LCD show that is utilized in numerous ventures to show some data to the client. Be that as it may, these LCD showcases have a huge deal of impediment in what they can do. In this instructional exercise, we will utilize OLED to show some fundamental data from the Android cell phone like Time, date, organize quality and battery status. This undertaking gives an essential thought and structure to assemble an Arduino based SmartWatch and can be additionally reached out to show approaching calls, messages as well as a lot more on OLED show.

So here we get some data from an Android cell phone by utilizing an android application and afterward send this data to OLED show by utilizing Bluetooth Module and Arduino Pro Mini. Android cell phone as of now has inbuilt Bluetooth to send the information and at accepting end we have utilized Bluetooth module HC-06 with Arduino. Bluetooth module HC-05 can likewise be utilized instead of HC-06.

In Android application, information is gotten from the cell phone as well as sent to the Arduino as a String. Presently subsequent to getting the information, Arduino deciphers the approaching series of bytes and put it in the impermanent factors to show it on OLED show. In OLED show we have made a few illustrations to demonstrate the qualities, get familiar with utilizing OLED show with Arduino here.

Hardware Required

1. Arduino (we have utilized Arduino Pro Mini. In any case, we can utilize any Arduino Board)
2. 128×64 OLED show Module (SSD1306)
3. Connecting Wires
4. Bluetooth HC05/HC06
5. 3.7v Li-On Battery
6. Jumper

Getting to know about OLED Displays

The term OLED means "Natural Light transmitting diode" it utilizes a similar innovation that is utilized in the vast majority of our TVs yet has less pixels contrasted with them. It is genuine amusing to have these cool looking presentation modules to be interfaced with the Arduino since it will make our ventures look cool. We have secured a full Article on OLED presentations and its sorts here. Here, we are utilizing a Monochrome 4-stick SSD1306 0.96" OLED show. This Display can just work with the I2C mode.

VCC -> 3.3v
GND -> GND
SDA -> SDA (Physical pin 3)
SCL -> SCL (Physical pin 5

Arduino people group has effectively given us a ton of Libraries which can be straightforwardly used to make this much easier. I evaluated a couple of libraries and found that the Adafruit_SSD1306 Library was anything but difficult to utilize and had a bunch of graphical choices henceforth we will utilize the equivalent in this didactic exercise. Here we additionally need to introduce one more library in Arduino IDE which can be downloaded from here GFX Graphics Library.

OLED looks cool and can be effectively interfaced with different microcontrollers to manufacture some intriguing activities:

- Interfacing SSD1306 OLED Display with Raspberry Pi

- Interfacing SSD1306 OLED Display with Arduino

- Web Clock utilizing ESP32 and OLED Display

- Programmed AC Temperature Controller utilizing Arduino, DHT11 and IR Blaster

Circuit Diagram

The Circuit Diagram for utilizing 4 stick SSD1306 OLED with Arduino is straightforward and is demonstrated as follows

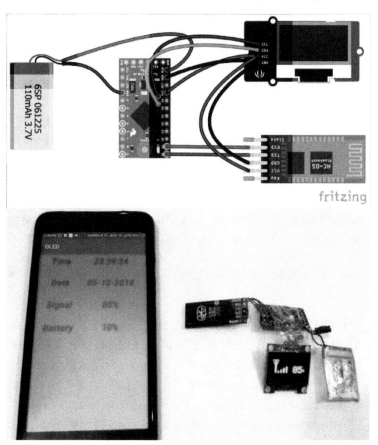

Here we have utilized an Arduino Pro Mini board to control every one of the activities. The motivation to pick Arduino star smaller than usual it can work at 3.3v power supply. The 4 stick OLED and Bluetooth module HC-06 can likewise take a shot at 3.3v, so these modules can be controlled by a solitary 3.7v Li-on. Li-on battery is the minimized and light weight battery, and is the ideal decision for wearable gadgets. Furthermore, here we likewise make something wearable in this undertaking like a straightforward smartwatch, which can be adjusted with your cell phone.

Presently one inquiry emerges about power supply is that here every one of the modules are dealing with 3.3v however li-particle battery is giving 3.7v which may harm the modules. So to tackle this issue we have connected battery's 3.7v supply to a crude stick of Arduino master scaled down which can change over that voltage to 3.3v.

Android App for sending data to Arduino over Bluetooth

For this Arduino based Smart Watch, we made an Android App in Android Studio, this application can be installed here. So simply download and introduce this application in your Android Smart telephone and afterward empower the Bluetooth and pair the HC-06 module with your telephone. It might request password to match the HC-06 bluetooth module, default password is 1234 or 0000.

Presently open the OLED application and select combined Bluetooth gadget HC-06, as appeared in the underneath picture:

Presently OLED application will show the information got from the android telephone as demonstrated as follows:

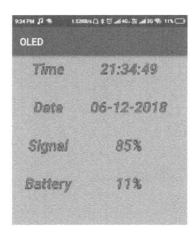

Programming Arduino for OLED Smart Watch

First download and the Adafruit Library and the GFX

library from Github utilizing the connections beneath

- Adafruit Library

- GFX Graphics Library

At that point start with including all the required libraries

```
#include<SoftwareSerial.h>

SoftwareSerial Serial1(10, 11);

#include <SPI.h>

#include <Wire.h>

#include <Adafruit_GFX.h>

#include "Adafruit_SSD1306.h"

#define OLED_RESET 4

Adafruit_SSD1306 display(OLED_RESET);
```

After this we have characterized a few macros and factors for various tasks.

```
#define NUMFLAKES 10

#define XPOS 0

#define YPOS 1

#define DELTAY 2

#define LOGO16_GLCD_HEIGHT 16

#define LOGO16_GLCD_WIDTH 16

String str = "";

byte h = 0;

byte m = 0;

byte S = 0;

String dmy, time, network, battery, inNumber, s;

byte centerX = 24;

byte centerY = 39;

byte Radius = 24;
```

```
double RAD = 3.141592 / 180;

double LR = 89.99;
```

After this compose a capacity for simple clock.

```
void showTimeAnalog(int center_x, int center_y,
double pl1, double pl2, double pl3)

{

  double x1, x2, y1, y2;

  x1 = center_x + (Radius * pl1) * cos((6 * pl3 + LR) *
RAD);

  y1 = center_y + (Radius * pl1) * sin((6 * pl3 + LR) *
RAD);

  x2 = center_x + (Radius * pl2) * cos((6 * pl3 - LR) *
RAD);

  y2 = center_y + (Radius * pl2) * sin((6 * pl3 - LR) *
RAD);

  display.drawLine((int)x1, (int)y1, (int)x2, (int)y2,
WHITE);

}
```

At that point there is another capacity for computerized Clock.

```
void digitalClock()

{

  display.setTextSize(1);

  display.setTextColor(WHITE);

  display.setCursor(60, 20);

  display.println(dmy);

  display.setTextSize(2);

  display.setCursor(60, 30);

  display.println(time);

  display.display();

  delay(2000);

}
```

At that point OLED will show the Battery status in Numeric and Graphic Forms utilizing the capacity beneath.

```
void Battery()

{

  display.clearDisplay();

  display.setTextSize(2);

  display.setTextColor(WHITE);

  display.setCursor(20, 0);
```

```
display.print("Bat:");

display.print(battery);

display.print("%");

display.drawRect(14, 20, 80, 40, WHITE);

display.drawRect(94, 30, 10, 20, WHITE);

display.fillRect(14, 20, (int)(8 * (battery.toInt()) /
10), 40, WHITE);

display.display();

delay(2000);

}
```

Underneath capacity is utilized for showing status of Network in Numeric and Graphic Form also.

```
void Network()

{

  display.clearDisplay();

  display.drawLine(5, 15, 25, 15, WHITE);

  display.drawLine(5, 15, 14, 30, WHITE);

  display.drawLine(25, 15, 17, 30, WHITE);

  display.fillRect(14, 15, 4, 40, WHITE);
```

```
int net = network.toInt() / 20;

int x1 = 24, y1 = 50, x2 = 4, y2 = 5;

........

.....
```

After that in arrangement work, we have initialiase all correspondences and modules that we have utilized in this task.

```
void setup()

{
```

```
  Serial.begin(9600);

  display.begin(SSD1306_SWITCHCAPVCC,
0x3C); // initialize with the I2C addr 0x3D (for the
128x64)

  display.clearDisplay();

  Serial1.begin(9600);

  Serial1.println("System Ready");

}
```

Also, in circle work, we have gotten information from android versatile and decoded that information and sent them to OLED show.

```
void loop(){

  Serial1.println("1234");

  delay(1000);

  while (Serial1.available() > 0){

    char ch = Serial1.read();

    str += ch;
```

```
if(ch == '$'){

    dmy = str.substring(str.indexOf("#") + 1, str.in-
dexOf(" "));

    time = str.substring(str.indexOf(" ") + 1, str.in-
dexOf(",") - 3);

    network = str.substring(str.indexOf(",") + 1,
str.indexOf(",,"));

    battery = str.substring(str.indexOf(",,") + 2,
str.indexOf(",,,"));

    inNumber = str.substring(str.indexOf(",,,") + 3,
str.indexOf("$"));

    s = time.substring(time.indexOf(" ") + 1,
time.indexOf(" ") + 3);

    h = s.toInt();

    s = time.substring(time.indexOf(" ") + 4,
time.indexOf(" ") + 6);

    m = s.toInt();

    s = time.substring(time.indexOf(" ") + 7,
time.indexOf(" ") + 9);
```

```
    S = s.toInt();

    str = "";}

 }

 display.clearDisplay();

 display.drawCircle(centerX,    centerY,    Radius,
WHITE);

 showTimeAnalog(centerX, centerY, 0.1, 0.5, h * 5
+ (int)(m * 5 / 60));

 showTimeAnalog(centerX, centerY, 0.1, 0.78, m);

 // showTimePin(centerX, centerY, 0.1, 0.9, S);

 digitalClock();

 Battery();

 Network();

}
```

This is the way we can associate OLED with and Smartphone remotely and can send or match up whatever information we need from the advanced cell to OLED.

Code

```
#include<SoftwareSerial.h>
SoftwareSerial Serial1(10, 11);

#include <SPI.h>
#include <Wire.h>
#include <Adafruit_GFX.h>
#include "Adafruit_SSD1306.h"

#define OLED_RESET 4
Adafruit_SSD1306 display(OLED_RESET);

#define NUMFLAKES 10
#define XPOS 0
#define YPOS 1
#define DELTAY 2

#define LOGO16_GLCD_HEIGHT 16
#define LOGO16_GLCD_WIDTH 16
String str = "";
byte h = 0;
byte m = 0;
byte S = 0;
String dmy, time, network, battery, inNumber, s;
byte centerX = 24;
byte centerY = 39;
byte Radius = 24;

double RAD = 3.141592 / 180;
double LR = 89.99;

void showTimeAnalog(int center_x, int center_y,
double pl1, double pl2, double pl3)
{
```

```
double x1, x2, y1, y2;
 x1 = center_x + (Radius * pl1) * cos((6 * pl3 + LR) *
RAD);
 y1 = center_y + (Radius * pl1) * sin((6 * pl3 + LR) * RAD);
 x2 = center_x + (Radius * pl2) * cos((6 * pl3 - LR) * RAD);
 y2 = center_y + (Radius * pl2) * sin((6 * pl3 - LR) * RAD);
   display.drawLine((int)x1, (int)y1, (int)x2, (int)y2,
WHITE);
}
void digitalClock()
{
 display.setTextSize(1);
 display.setTextColor(WHITE);
 display.setCursor(60, 20);
 display.println(dmy);
 display.setTextSize(2);
 display.setCursor(60, 30);
 display.println(time);
 display.display();
 delay(2000);
}
void Battery()
{
 display.clearDisplay();
 display.setTextSize(2);
 display.setTextColor(WHITE);
 display.setCursor(20, 0);
 display.print("Bat:");
 display.print(battery);
 display.print("%");
```

```
display.drawRect(14, 20, 80, 40, WHITE);
display.drawRect(94, 30, 10, 20, WHITE);
display.fillRect(14, 20, (int)(8 * (battery.toInt()) / 10),
40, WHITE);
display.display();
delay(2000);
}
void Network()
{
display.clearDisplay();
display.drawLine(5, 15, 25, 15, WHITE);
display.drawLine(5, 15, 14, 30, WHITE);
display.drawLine(25, 15, 17, 30, WHITE);
display.fillRect(14, 15, 4, 40, WHITE);
int net = network.toInt() / 20;
int x1 = 24, y1 = 50, x2 = 4, y2 = 5;
for (int i = 1; i <= net; i++)
{
 display.fillRect(x1, y1, x2, y2, WHITE);
 x1 += 10;
 y1 -= 5;
 y2 += 10;
 y2 -= 5;
}
display.setTextSize(3);
display.setTextColor(WHITE);
display.setCursor(80, 34);
display.print(network);
display.setTextSize(1);
display.setCursor(117, 44);
```

```
display.println("%");
display.display();
delay(2000);
}
void setup()
{
Serial.begin(9600);
 display.begin(SSD1306_SWITCHCAPVCC, 0x3C);  //
initialize with the I2C addr 0x3D (for the 128x64)
display.clearDisplay();
Serial1.begin(9600);
Serial1.println("System Ready");
}
void loop(){
Serial1.println("1234");
delay(1000);
while (Serial1.available() > 0){
 char ch = Serial1.read();
 str += ch;
 if(ch == '$'){
     dmy = str.substring(str.indexOf("#") + 1, str.in-
dexOf(" "));
     time = str.substring(str.indexOf(" ") + 1, str.in-
dexOf(",") - 3);
   network = str.substring(str.indexOf(",") + 1, str.in-
dexOf(",,"));
     battery = str.substring(str.indexOf(",,") + 2, str.in-
dexOf(",,,"));
      inNumber = str.substring(str.indexOf(",,,") + 3,
str.indexOf("$"));
```

```
    s = time.substring(time.indexOf(" ") + 1, time.in-
dexOf(" ") + 3);
  h = s.toInt();
    s = time.substring(time.indexOf(" ") + 4, time.in-
dexOf(" ") + 6);
  m = s.toInt();
    s = time.substring(time.indexOf(" ") + 7, time.in-
dexOf(" ") + 9);
  S = s.toInt();
  str = "";}
}
 display.clearDisplay();
    display.drawCircle(centerX,   centerY,   Radius,
WHITE);
 showTimeAnalog(centerX, centerY, 0.1, 0.5, h * 5 +
(int)(m * 5 / 60));
 showTimeAnalog(centerX, centerY, 0.1, 0.78, m);
 // showTimePin(centerX, centerY, 0.1, 0.9, S);
 digitalClock();
 Battery();
 Network();
}
```

3.DIY WAVEFORM GENERATOR USING ARDUINO

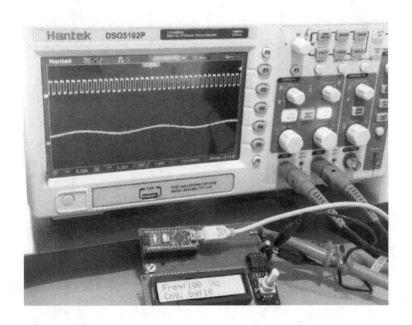

Each Engineer who wants to tinker with hardware eventually of time would need to have their own lab set-up. A Multimeter, Clamp meter, Oscilloscope, LCR Meter, Function Generator, Dual mode power supply and an Auto transformer are the absolute minimum types of gear for a better than average lab set-up. While these can be obtained, we can likewise effectively fabricated few all alone like the Function Generator and the Dual mode power supply.

In this article we will figure out how rapidly and effectively we can construct our very own Function generator utilizing Arduino. This capacity generator a.k.a waveform generator can create square wave (5V/0V) with recurrence going from 1Hz to 2MHz, the recurrence of the wave can be constrained by a handle and the obligation cycle is hardcoded to half yet it is anything but difficult to change that in the program too. Aside from that, the generator can likewise deliver since wave with recurrence control. Take note of this generator isn't of mechanical evaluation and can't be utilized for genuine testing. In any case, other than that it will prove to be useful for all leisure activity ventures and you need not trust that the shipment will arrive. Additionally what's better time than utilizing a gadget, that we based alone.

Materials Required

1. Arduino Nano
2. Rotary Encoder

3. 16*2 Alphanumeric LCD display
4. Capacitor (0.1uF)
5. Resistor(5.6K,10K)
6. Perfboard, Bergstik
7. Soldering Kit

Circuit Diagram

The total circuit outline this Arduino Function Generator is demonstrated as follows. As should be obvious we have an Arduino Nano which goes about as the mind of our undertaking and a 16x2 LCD to show the estimation of recurrence that is at present being created. We additionally have a revolving encoder which will assist us with setting the recurrence.

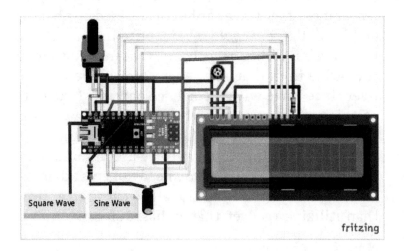

The total set-up is controlled by the USB port of the Arduino itself. The associations which I utilized already didn't finish working duty to certain reasons which we will examine later in this article. Henceforth I needed to wreckage up with the wiring a piece by changing the stick request. At any rate, you won't have any such issues as it is altogether dealt with, simply pursue the circuit cautiously to realize which stick is interface with what. Likewise you can allude the underneath table to confirm your associations.

Arduino Pin	Connected to
D14	Connected to RS of LCD
D15	Connected to RN of LCD
D4	Connected to D4 of LCD
D3	Connected to D5 of LCD
D6	Connected to D6 of LCD
D7	Connected to D7 of LCD
D10	Connect to Rotary Encoder 2
D11	Connect to Rotary Encoder 3
D12	Connect to Rotary Encoder 4
D9	Outputs square wave
D2	Connect to D9 of Arduino
D5	Outputs SPWM then converted to

	sine

The circuit is really straightforward; we produce a square wave on stick D9 which can be utilized thusly, the recurrence of this square wave is constrained by the turning encoder. At that point to get a sine wave we produce SPWM signal on stick D5, the recurrence of this must be connected with PWM recurrence so we give this PWM sign to stick D2 to go about as a hinder and afterward utilize the ISR to control the recurrence of the since wave.

You can fabricate the circuit on a breadboard or even get a PCB for it. Be that as it may, I chose to weld it on a Perf board to complete the work quick and make it solid for long haul use. My board resembles this once every one of the associations are finished.

In the event that you need to know more on how the PWM and Sine wave is created with Arduino read the accompanying passages, else you can look down legitimately to the Programming Arduino segment.

Producing Square Wave with Variable Frequency

Individuals who are utilizing Arduino may be well-known that Arduino can deliver PWM flag just by utilizing the simple compose work. Be that as it may, this capacity is constrained distinctly to control the obligation cycle of the PWM signal and not the recurrence of the sign. Be that as it may, for a waveform generator we need a PWM signal whose recurrence can be controlled. This should be possible by legitimately controlling the Timers of the Arduino and flipping a GPIO stick dependent on it. As it may, there are some pre-fabricated libraries which do notwithstanding and can be utilized all things considered. The library that we are utilizing is the Arduino PWM Frequency Library. We will examine progressively about this library in the coding area.

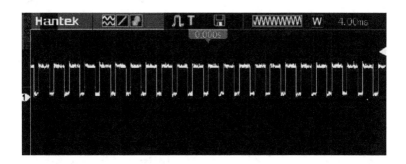

There are a some downsides with this library also, on the grounds that the library adjusts the default Timer 1 and Timer 2 settings in Arduino. Consequently you will never again have the option to utilize servo library or some other clock related library with your Arduino. Additionally the simple compose work on pins 9,10,11 and 13 uses Timer 1 and Timer 2 subsequently you won't almost certainly produce SPWM on those pins.

The benefit of this library is, it doesn't exasperate the Timer 0 of your Arduino, which is more fundamental than Timer 1 and Timer 2. In view of this you are permitted to utilize the postpone work and millis() work with no issue. Additionally the pins 5 and 6 are constrained by Timer 0 thus we won't have issue in utilizing simple compose or servo control activity on those pins. At first it required some investment for me to make sense of one or the other is the reason the wiring is wrecked a piece.

Here we have likewise constructed one Simple Square waveform generator, however to change the recurrence of waveform you need to supplant Resistor or capacitor, and it will hard to get the required recurrence.

Producing Sine Wave using Arduino

As we probably am aware microcontrollers are Digital gadgets and they can't deliver Sine wave by unimportant coding. In any case, there two famous methods for acquiring a sine wave from a microcontroller one is by using a DAC and the other is by making a SPWM. Tragically Arduino sheets (aside from

Due) does not accompany an implicit DAC to create sine wave, however you can generally construct your very own DAC utilizing the straightforward R2R strategy and afterward use it to deliver a better than average sine wave. Be that as it may, to diminish the equipment work I chose to utilize the later strategy for making a SPWM sign and afterward changing over it to Sine wave.

What is a SPWM signal?

The term SPWM represents Sinusoidal Pulse Width Modulation. This sign is particularly like the PWM, however for a SPWM signal the obligation cycle is controlled in this way to acquire a normal voltage like that of a sine wave. For instance, with 100% obligation cycle the normal yield voltage will be 5V and for 25% we will have 1.25V along these lines controlling the obligation cycle we can get pre-characterized variable normal voltage which is only a sine wave. This procedure is generally utilized in Inverters.

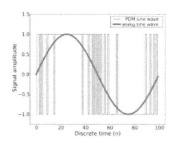

In the above picture, the blue sign is the SPWM signal. Notice that the obligation cycle of the wave is changed from 0% to 100% and after that back to 0%. The diagram is plotted for - 1.0 to +1.0V however for our situation, since we are utilizing an Arduino the scale will be structure 0V to 5V. We will find out how to deliver SPWM with Arduino in the programming segment underneath.

Converting SPWM to Sine wave

Changing over a SPWM single to sine wave need a H-connect circuit which comprises of least 4 power switches. We won't go a lot further into it since we are not utilizing it here. These H-connect circuits are generally utilized in inverters. It uses two SPWM signals where one is stage moved from the other and both the sign are connected to the power switches in the H-scaffold to make corner to corner contradicting switches turn on and off and a similar time. Along these lines we can get a wave structure that appears to be like sine wave yet will for all intents and purposes not be nearer to anything appeared in the figure above (green wave). To get an unadulterated since wave yield we need to utilize a channel like the low-pass channel which contains an Inductor and Capacitor.

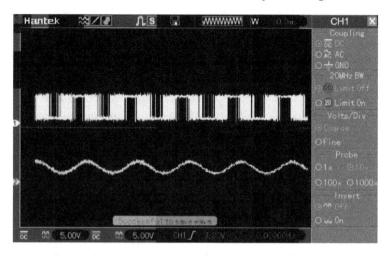

Anyway in our circuit, we won't utilize the sine wave to control anything. I just needed to make from the produced SPWM signal so I went with a straightforward RC-Filter. You can likewise attempt a LC-Filter for better outcomes however I picked RC for effortlessness. The estimation of my resistor is 620 Ohms and the capacitor is 10uF. The above picture demonstrates the SPWM signal (Yellow) from the stick 5 and the sine wave (Blue) which was gotten in the wake of going it through a RC-Filter.

In case you would prefer not to fluctuate the recurrence, you can likewise produce sine wave by utilizing this Simple Sine Wave Generator Circuit utilizing Transistor.

Adding the Arduino PWM Frequency Library

The Arduino Frequency Library can be downloaded

by tapping on the connection underneath.

- Arduino PWM Frequency Library

At the hour of composing this article, the Arduino PWM Frequency Librarey V_05 is the most recent one as well as it will get installed as a ZIP document. Concentrate the ZIP record advertisement you will get an organizer called PWM. At that point explore to the Libraries organizer of your Arduino IDE, for windows clients it will be in your records at this way C:\Users \User\Documents\Arduino\libraries. Glue the PWM organizer into the libraries envelope. Sometimes you may as of now have a PWM organizer in there, all things considered ensure you supplant the former one with this new one.

Programming Arduino for Waveform Generator

As consistently the total program for this task can be found at the base of this page. You can utilize the code all things considered, yet ensure you have included the variable recurrence library for Arduino IDE as talked about above else you will get accumulate time mistake. In this area we should look in to the code to comprehend what's going on.

Fundamentally we need to deliver a PWM signal with variable recurrence on stick 9. This recurrence ought to be set utilizing the revolving encoder and the worth ought to likewise be shown in the 16*2 LCD.

When the PWM sign is made on stick 9 it will make a hinder on stick 2 since we have shorted both the pins. Utilizing this intrude on we can control the recurrence of the SPWM signal which is produced on stick 5.

As consistently we start our program by including the required library. The fluid precious stone library is in-worked in Arduino and we just introduced the PWM library.

```
#include <PWM.h> //PWM librarey for controlling freq. of PWM signal

#include <LiquidCrystal.h>
```

Next we announce the worldwide variable and furthermore notice the stick names for the LCD, Rotary Encoder and sign pins. You can leave this undisturbed in case you have pursued the circuit outline above.

```
const int rs = 14, en = 15, d4 = 4, d5 = 3, d6 = 6, d7 = 7; //Mention the pin number

for LCD connection

LiquidCrystal lcd(rs, en, d4, d5, d6, d7);
```

```
const int Encoder_OuputA = 11;

const int Encoder_OuputB = 12;

const int Encoder_Switch = 10;

const int signal_pin = 9;

const int Sine_pin = 5;

const int POT_pin = A2;

int Previous_Output;

int multiplier = 1;

double angle = 0;

double increment = 0.2;

int32_t frequency; //frequency to be set

int32_t lower_level_freq = 1; //Lowest possible
freq value is 1Hz

int32_t upper_level_freq = 100000; //Maximum
possible freq is 100KHz
```

Inside the arrangement work we instate the LCD and sequential correspondence for investigating reason and after that announce the pins of Encoder as information pins. We likewise show an introduction message during the boot just to ensure things are working.

```
lcd.begin(16, 2); //Initialise 16*2 LCD

lcd.print("Signal Generator"); //Intro Message
line 1

lcd.setCursor(0, 1);

lcd.print("-Hello"); //Intro Message line 2

delay(2000);

lcd.clear();

lcd.print("Freq:00000Hz");

lcd.setCursor(0, 1);

lcd.print("Inc. by: 1 ");

Serial.begin(9600); //Serial for debugging

//pin Mode declaration

pinMode (Encoder_OuputA, INPUT);
```

```
pinMode (Encoder_OuputB, INPUT);

pinMode (Encoder_Switch, INPUT);
```

Another significant line is the InitTimerSafe which introduces the clock 1 and 2 for creating a variable recurrence PWM. When this capacity is known as the default clock settings of Arduino will be adjusted.

```
InitTimersSafe(); //Initialize timers without dis-
turbing timer 0
```

We likewise have the outer interfere with running on stick 2. So at whatever point there an adjustment in status of stick 2 a hinder will be activated which will run the Interrupt administration routine (ISR) work. Here the name of the ISR capacity is generate_sine.

```
attachInterrupt(0,generate_sine,CHANGE);
```

Next, inside the void circle we must check if the revolving encoder has been turned. Just in the event that it has been turned we have to modify the recurrence of the PWM signal. We have as of now figured out how to interface Rotary Encoder with Arduino. In the event that you are new here I would prescribe you to fall back to that instructional exercise and after that get back here.

In the event that the rotating encoder is turned clockwise we increment the estimation of recurrence by including it with the estimation of multiplier. Thusly we can expand/decline the estimation of recurrence by 1, 10, 100 or even 1000. The estimation of multiplier can be set by squeezing the turning encoder. In the event that the encoder is turned we adjust the estimation of recurrence and produce a PWM signal on stick 9 with the accompanying lines. Here the worth 32768 sets the PWM to half cycle. The worth 32768 is picked, since half of 65536 is 32768 correspondingly you can decide the incentive for your required obligation cycles. In any case, here the obligation cycle is fixed to half. Finally the capacity SetPinFrequencySafe is utilized to set the recurrence of our sign stick that is stick 9.

```
pwmWriteHR(signal_pin, 32768); //Set duty
cycle to 50% by default -> for 16-bit 65536/2 =
32768

SetPinFrequencySafe(signal_pin, frequency);
```

Inside the ISR work we compose the code to create SPWM signal. There are numerous approaches to create SPWM flag and even pre-assembled libraries are accessible for Arduino. I have utilized the least complex of all strategies for using the transgression() work in Arduino. You can likewise attempt with the query table technique in case you are intrigued. The transgression() restores a variable worth (decimal) between - 1 to +1 and this when plotted against time will give us a sine wave.

Presently we should simply change over this estimation of - 1 to +1 into 0 to 255 and feed it to our simple Write work. For which I have increased it with 255 just to overlook the decimal point and after that utilized the guide capacity to change over the incentive from - 255 to +255 into 0 to +255. At last this worth is composed to stick 5 utilizing the simple compose work. The estimation of point is increased by 0.2 each time the ISR is called this assistance us in controlling the recurrence of the sine wave

```
double sineValue = sin(angle);

  sineValue *= 255;

  int plot = map(sineValue, -255, +255, 0, 255);

  Serial.println(plot);

  analogWrite(Sine_pin,plot);

  angle += increment;
```

Testing the Arduino Function Generator on Hardware

Manufacture your equipment according to the circuit outline and transfer the code given at the base of this page. Presently, you are good to go to test your undertaking. It would be significantly simpler in case you have a DSO (Oscilloscope) however you can likewise test it with a LED since the recurrence range is high.

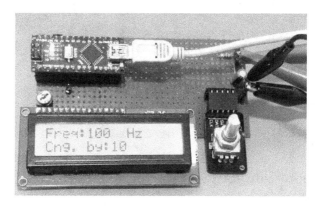

Associate the test to the Square wave and sine wave stick of the circuit. Utilize two LEDs on these two pins on the off chance that you don't have an extension. Catalyst the circuit and you ought to be welcomed with the basic message on the LCD. At that point differ the Rotary encoder and set the required recurrence you ought to have the option to watch the square wave and sine wave on your extension as demonstrated as follows. In case you are utilizing a LED you should see the LED flickering at various interims dependent on the recurrence you have set.

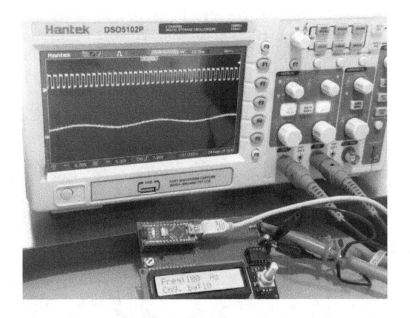

Expectation you appreciated the undertaking and took in something valuable from it.

Code

```
#include <PWM.h> //PWM librarey for controlling freq. of PWM signal
#include <LiquidCrystal.h>
const int rs = 14, en = 15, d4 = 4, d5 = 3, d6 = 6, d7 = 7; // Mention the pin number for LCD connection
```

```
LiquidCrystal lcd(rs, en, d4, d5, d6, d7);
int Encoder_OuputA = 11;
int Encoder_OuputB = 12;
int Encoder_Switch = 10;
int Previous_Output;
int multiplier = 1;
double angle = 0;
double increment = 0.2;
const int signal_pin = 9;
const int Sine_pin = 5;
const int POT_pin = A2;
int32_t frequency; //frequency to be set
int32_t lower_level_freq = 1; //Lowest possible freq
value is 1Hz
int32_t upper_level_freq = 100000; //Maximum pos-
sible freq is 100KHz
void setup()
{
 lcd.begin(16, 2); //Initialise 16*2 LCD
 lcd.print("Signal Generator"); //Intro Message line 1
 lcd.setCursor(0, 1);
 lcd.print("-Hello "); //Intro Message line 2
 delay(2000);
 lcd.clear();
 lcd.print("Freq:00000Hz");
 lcd.setCursor(0, 1);
 lcd.print("Inc. by: 1 ");


 Serial.begin(9600); //Serial for debugging
```

```
  InitTimersSafe(); //Initialize timers without dis-
turbing timer 0


//pin Mode declaration
 pinMode (Encoder_OuputA, INPUT);
 pinMode (Encoder_OuputB, INPUT);
 pinMode (Encoder_Switch, INPUT);
    Previous_Output  =  digitalRead(Encoder_Ou-
putA); //Read the inital value of Output A
attachInterrupt(0,generate_sine,CHANGE);
}
void loop()
{
  if (digitalRead(Encoder_OuputA) != Previous_Out-
put)
  {
   if (digitalRead(Encoder_OuputB) != Previous_Out-
put)
   {
   frequency = frequency + multiplier;
   // Serial.println(frequency);
   pwmWriteHR(signal_pin, 32768); //Set duty cycle
to 50% by default -> for 16-bit 65536/2 = 32768
   SetPinFrequencySafe(signal_pin, frequency);
   lcd.setCursor(0, 0);
   lcd.print("Freq:   Hz");
   lcd.setCursor(5, 0);
   lcd.print(frequency);
   }
```

```
  else
  {
   frequency = frequency -  multiplier;
   // Serial.println(frequency);
   pwmWriteHR(signal_pin, 32768); //Set duty cycle
to 50% by default -> for 16-bit 65536/2 = 32768
   SetPinFrequencySafe(signal_pin, frequency);
   lcd.setCursor(0, 0);
   lcd.print("Freq:   Hz");
   lcd.setCursor(5, 0);
   lcd.print(frequency);
  }
 }
  if(digitalRead(Encoder_Switch) == 0)
  {
  multiplier = multiplier * 10;
  if(multiplier>1000)
  multiplier=1;


  // Serial.println(multiplier);
  lcd.setCursor(0, 1);
  lcd.print("Cng. by:   ");
  lcd.setCursor(8, 1);
  lcd.print(multiplier);


   delay(500);
  while(digitalRead(Encoder_Switch) == 0);
  }
```

```
  Previous_Output = digitalRead(Encoder_OuputA);


}
void generate_sine()
{
  double sineValue = sin(angle);
  sineValue *= 255;
  int plot = map(sineValue, -255, +255, 0, 255);
  Serial.println(plot);
  analogWrite(Sine_pin,plot);
  angle += increment;
  if(angle > 180)
  angle =0;
}
```

4.HOW TO USE BLUETOOTH WITH MATLAB FOR WIRELESS COMMUNICATION

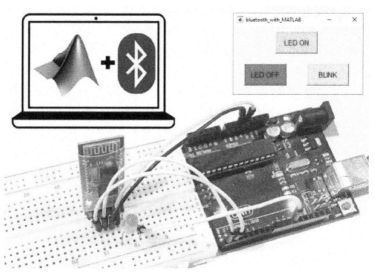

Bluetooth is the easiest and most well known convention for short extend remote correspondence in implanted frameworks. Bluetooth isn't utilized for moving the information starting with one gadget then the next yet additionally used to control the gadgets remotely. Pretty much every electronic device has Bluetooth bolster now days so it is savvy decision to have Bluetooth control choice in your inserted application.

In this didactical exercise, we will figure out how to utilize Bluetooth in MATLAB to convey remotely. We will utilize PC's in-constructed Bluetooth with MATLAB at one side and HC-05 with Arduino at opposite side. There are 2 ways to arrangement correspondence among MATLAB and Arduino by means of Bluetooth, one is utilizing direction window and other is utilizing MATLAB GUI. The Arduino code for both the strategies will continue as before. In the event that you are new to MATLAB, at that point it is prescribed to begin with basic LED flicker program with MATLAB and become familiar with the fundamental phrasing utilized in MATLAB. You can further investigate more MATLAB Projects:

- Sequential Communication among MATLAB and Arduino

- DC Motor Manage Using MATLAB as well as Arduino

- Stepper Motor Control utilizing MATLAB and Arduino

- Beginning with Image Processing utilizing MATLAB

Components Required

- Arduino UNO
- MATLAB installed Laptop (Preference: R2016a or above versions)
- LED (any color)
- Bluetooth Module (HC-05)
- Jumper Wires
- Resistor (330 ohm)

To become familiar with HC-05 and its interfacing with Arduino, check the accompanying articles.

- Bluetooth Managed Servo Motor utilizing Arduino

- Voice Controlled LEDs utilizing Arduino and Bluetooth

- Phone Controlled AC utilizing Arduino and Bluetooth

Circuit Diagram

Schematics for Bluetooth correspondence among MATLAB and Arduino is given beneath:

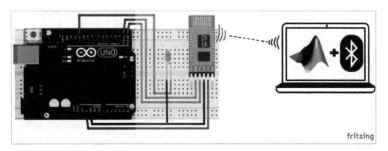

Bluetooth Communication using MATLAB Command Window

This is the basic strategy to arrangement Bluetooth correspondence among Arduino and MATLAB. Here, the MATLAB utilizes the workstation's bluetooth to associate HC-05 associated with Arduino. First we need to code the Arduino to peruse the sequential approaching information originating from the MATLAB (utilizing Laptop's Bluetooth).

At that point this Bluetooth transmitted information from MATLAB can be utilized to control anything associated with the Arduino. Here we have associated a LED to Arduino that can be controlled from the LAPTOP utilizing MATLAB.

In the first place, transfer the given Arduino code in the Arduino UNO and afterward start coding in MATLAB Command Window.

```
#include <SoftwareSerial.h>
```

```
int TxD;

int RxD;

int data;

SoftwareSerial bluetooth(TxD, RxD);

void setup() {

  Serial.begin(9600);

  bluetooth.begin(9600);

}

void loop()

{

if(bluetooth.available() > 0)

{

data = bluetooth.read();

Serial.print(data);

Serial.print("\n");
```

```
if(data == '1')

{

digitalWrite(11, HIGH);

}

else if(data == '0')

{

digitalWrite(11, LOW);

}

}

}
```

At that point, reorder the beneath MATLAB code in the Command window for Bluetooth correspondence among MATLAB and Arduino.

```
instrhwinfo('Bluetooth','HC-05');

bt = Bluetooth('HC-05', 1);

fopen(bt);
```

```
Command Window
   >> instrhwinfo('Bluetooth','HC-05');
   bt = Bluetooth('HC-05', 1);
   fopen(bt);
fx >>
```

In the beneath code, direction fprintf(bt,'0') is utilized to mood killer the LED by sending '0' to the Arduino. Presently, in case you need to turn ON the LED simply send '1' rather than '0' utilizing the underneath order.

fprintf(bt,'1');

```
Command Window
   >> instrhwinfo('Bluetooth','HC-05');
   bt = Bluetooth('HC-05', 1);
   fopen(bt);
   >> fprintf(bt,'1');
   >> fprintf(bt,'0');
fx >>
```

To check the data about the accessible equipment, use beneath order

instrhwinfo('type','Name of device');

To open the bluetooth port, beneath order in utilized

fopen(bt);

Bluetooth Communication using MATLAB GUI

For exhibiting Bluetooth Communication utilizing MATLAB GUI, we will make three graphical catches in MATLAB to turn on, turn off and flicker the LED associated with the Arduino. Information will be sent through bluetooth from MATLAB to HC-05 on tapping on those graphical catches. Arduino contains the code to get the Bluetooth transmitted information from MATLAB to HC-05 as well as managing the LED by information got. Arduino code will stay same as past one, just contrast is that, already we were sending information '1' and '0' through order window of MATLAB, and now similar information will be sent on tapping on three graphical catches.

To dispatch the GUI, type the beneath direction in the order window

guide

A popup window will open, at that point select new clear GUI as appeared in beneath picture,

Presently pick three pushbuttons for turning ON, OFF and Blink the LED, as demonstrated as follows,

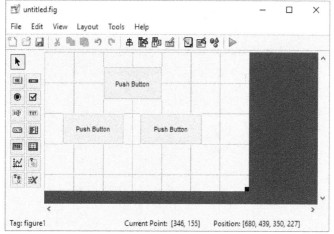

To resize or modify the state of the pushbuttons, simply click on it and you will almost certainly drag the

edges of the catch. By double tapping on pushbutton you can change the shading, string and tag of that specific catch. We have tweaked three pushbuttons as appeared in beneath picture.

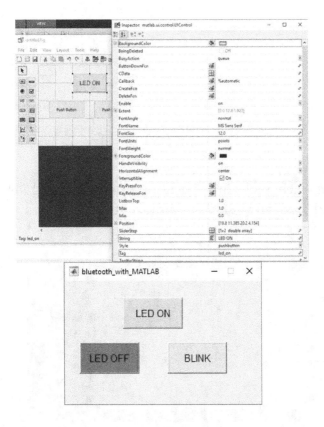

You can alter the catches according to your decision. Presently when you spare this, a code will be created in the Editor window of MATLAB. Alter this code as indicated by the undertaking you need to perform by your Arduino on getting Bluetooth information utilizing the MATLAB GUI. So underneath we have altered the MATLAB code. You can get familiar with Command window, proofreader window and so forth in Getting initiated with MATLAB instructional exercise.

Complete MATLAB code, for controlling LED from MATLAB by means of Bluetooth, is given toward the part of the bargain. Further we are including the GUI document (.fig) and code file(.m) here for download, utilizing which you can modify the catches according to your prerequisite. The following are a few changes we accomplished for controlling the LED associated with Arduino.

Reorder the underneath code on line no. 74 to arrangement or associate the MATLAB to the Laptop's Bluetooth.

```
clear All;

global bt;

instrhwinfo('Bluetooth','HC-05');

bt = Bluetooth('HC-05', 1);

fopen(bt);
```

```
72        % Get default command line output from handles structure
73 -      varargout{1} = handles.output;
74 -      clear All;
75 -      global bt;
76 -      instrhwinfo('Bluetooth','HC-05');
77 -      bt = Bluetooth('HC-05', 1);
78 -      fopen(bt);
```

where, fopen(bt) is utilized to open the Bluetooth port for transmitting information.

Presently, when you look down, you will see that there are three capacities made for three pushbuttons in the GUI. Presently compose the code in the capacities as indicated by the assignment you need to perform on snap.

In LED ON catch's capacity, reorder the beneath code just before the part of the bargain to turn ON the LED. In beneath code, fprintf(bt,'1') is utilized for sending '1' from MATLAB to HC-05 utilizing workstation's Bluetooth. Arduino will get this information '1' through HC-05 and sparkle the LED by making its eleventh stick HIGH.

```
global bt;

fprintf(bt,'1');
```

```
80      % --- Executes on button press in led_on.
81    ☐function led_on_Callback(hObject, eventdata, handles)
82    ☐% hObject      handle to led_on (see GCBO)
83     % eventdata  reserved - to be defined in a future version of MATLAB
84     % handles     structure with handles and user data (see GUIDATA)
85 -    global bt;
86 -    fprintf(bt,'1');
```

In LED OFF catch's capacity, reorder the underneath code just before the part of the arrangement to mood killer the LED. In beneath code, fprintf(bt,'0') is utilized for sending '0' from MATLAB to HC-05 utilizing PC's Bluetooth. Arduino will get '0' through HC-05 and mood killer the LED by making its eleventh stick LOW.

global bt;

fprintf(bt,'0');

```
89      % --- Executes on button press in led_off.
90    ☐function led_off_Callback(hObject, eventdata, handles)
91    ☐% hObject      handle to led_off (see GCBO)
92     % eventdata  reserved - to be defined in a future version of MATLAB
93     % handles     structure with handles and user data (see GUIDATA)
94 -    global bt;
95 -    fprintf(bt,'0');
```

In BLINK catch's capacity, utilize the underneath code to flicker the LED. A for circle is utilized to squint the LED multiple times.

global bt;

```
for i = 1:10

    fprintf(bt,'1');

    pause(0.5);

    fprintf(bt,'0');

    pause(0.5);

end
```

```
97      % --- Executes on button press in blink.
98      function blink_Callback(hObject, eventdata, handles)
99      % hObject    handle to blink (see GCBO)
100     % eventdata  reserved - to be defined in a future version of MATLAB
101     % handles    structure with handles and user data (see GUIDATA)
102 -   global bt;
103 -   for i = 1:10
104 -       fprintf(bt,'1');
105 -       pause(0.5);
106 -       fprintf(bt,'0');
107 -       pause(0.5);
108 -   end
```

In the wake of finishing with MATLAB GUI coding and arrangement the equipment as per circuit chart, simply click on the run catch to run the altered code in .m document.

MATLAB may take few moments to react, don't tap on any GUI catch until MATLAB shows BUSY sign, which you can see at the left base corner of the screen as demonstrated as follows,

When everything is prepared, click on LED-ON, LED OFF and BLINK catch to turn ON, OFF and Blink the LED separately. All the code documents for this venture can be downloaded from here or you can utilize the code given underneath.

Code

Arduino Code:

```
#include <SoftwareSerial.h>
int TxD;
int RxD;
int data;
SoftwareSerial bluetooth(TxD, RxD);
void setup() {
 Serial.begin(9600);
 bluetooth.begin(9600);
}
```

```
void loop()
{
if(bluetooth.available() > 0)
{
data = bluetooth.read();
if(data == '1')
digitalWrite(11, HIGH);
else if(data == '0')
digitalWrite(11, LOW);
}
}
```

Code for Bluetooth Communication using MATLAB Command Window

```
instrhwinfo('Bluetooth','HC-05');
bt = Bluetooth('HC-05', 1);
fopen(bt);
fprintf(bt,'1');
fprintf(bt,'0');
```

Code for Bluetooth Communication using MATLAB GUI

```
gui_Singleton = 1;
gui_State = struct('gui_Name',    mfilename, ...
        'gui_Singleton', gui_Singleton, ...
            'gui_OpeningFcn', @bluetooth_with_MAT-
LAB_OpeningFcn, ...
            'gui_OutputFcn', @bluetooth_with_MAT-
LAB_OutputFcn, ...
        'gui_LayoutFcn', [], ...
        'gui_Callback', []);
```

```
if nargin && ischar(varargin{1})
  gui_State.gui_Callback = str2func(varargin{1});
end
if nargout
    [varargout{1:nargout}] = gui_mainfcn(gui_State,
varargin{:});
else
  gui_mainfcn(gui_State, varargin{:});
end
function        bluetooth_with_MATLAB_OpeningFc-
n(hObject, eventdata, handles, varargin)
function varargout = bluetooth_with_MATLAB_Out-
putFcn(hObject, eventdata, handles)
varargout{1} = handles.output;
clear All;
global bt;
instrhwinfo('Bluetooth','HC-05');
bt = Bluetooth('HC-05', 1);
fopen(bt);
function led_on_Callback(hObject, eventdata, han-
dles)
global bt;
fprintf(bt,'1');
function led_off_Callback(hObject, eventdata, han-
dles)
global bt;
fprintf(bt,'0');
```

Anbazhagan k

```
function blink_Callback(hObject, eventdata, handles)
global bt;
for i = 1:10
  fprintf(bt,'1');
  pause(0.5);
  fprintf(bt,'0');
  pause(0.5);
end
```

5.HOW TO BURN ARDUINO BOOTLOADER IN ATEMGA328 IC AND PROGRAM IT USING ARDUINO IDE

We as a whole realize that, Atmega328 IC is utilized in Arduino UNO board. This IC is the cerebrum of the Arduino board. In reality, Arduino architects needed to make a helpful prototyping board for the amateurs so they composed every one of the segments in such manner that anyone can get to every one of the pins of the Atmega328 IC and can program it just by interfacing it to PC. Arduino board is famous for structure leisure activity ventures. Be that as it may, in modern or customer items its not smart thought to utilize the total Arduino board, so we can utilize independent Atmega328 IC, which can be modified with Arduino IDE however without utilizing Arduino board.

In this instructional exercise, we will perceive how supplant Arduino board with Atmega328 IC and with couple of different parts. For utilizing Atmega328 IC instead of arduino, first we need to consume Arduino Bootloader in it and after that we will program it utilizing FTDI or utilizing Arduino Board. This instructional exercise will likewise help in supplanting harmed Atmega328 IC from Arduino board. Likewise by utilizing the circuit portrayed underneath you can construct your own Arduino board by imitating it on PCB.

Components Required

     1. Atmega 328 IC
     2. Breadboard
     3. LM7805
     4. 22pF ceramic capacitors (2)
     5. 16 MHz Crystal
     6. 10 K resistor
     7. 10uF capacitor(2)
     8. Jumper wires
     9. 1k resistor

Alternatively, you can likewise utilize 3.3v voltage controller LM1117-3.3v to incorporate 3.3v rail in your circuit.

Pin Diagram of Atmega328

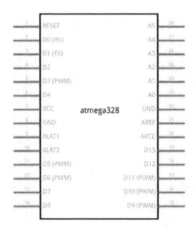

Circuit Diagram

Circuit Diagram for recreating Arduino on Breadboard is given beneath:

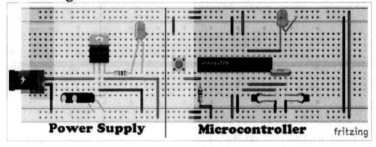

Component Descriptions

Power supply part-

1. **5V voltage regulator:** Atmega 328 IC keeps running on 5V power supply. Here, we are utilizing LM7805 to get 5v yield, it can deal with

upto 30V as information. In case you have a different 5V supply, at that point You can leave this progression.

2. **Capacitors:**10uF capacitor is utilized at the info and yield some portion of 7805 to side-step any AC segment to ground.

3. **LED:** This will show you that your 5V output is coming.

Microcontroller part-

1. **Atmega 328:** This is our principle segment on the breadboard. Its stick chart is given above.

2. **Crystal oscillator:** A 16MHz outside precious stone is associated between Pin 9 and Pin 10 of the ATmega328. This precious stone is utilized to offer clock to the microcontroller to execute the undertakings quicker.

3. **Push Button:** To reset the microcontroller a push catch is associated between stick 1 and GND. Typically, it is associated with 5v utilizing a 10k resistor.

4. **LED:** A drove is associated with advanced stick 13.

This total instructional exercise is isolated into three

sections to make your own Arduino running on breadboard:

1. Building the Arduino Circuit on Breadboard

2. Consuming the Bootloader into Atmega328 IC

3. Step by step instructions to Program Arduino Bootloader transferred Atmega 328 IC on breadboard.

Presently we will clarify each section individually.

Part-1: Building the Arduino Circuit on Breadboard

Stage 1:- Connect the Power Supply Part as appeared in circuit graph and test it utilizing outer power supply to LM7805. It will resembles this.

Stage 2:- Now, interface the Microcontroller Part as appeared in circuit chart. Make the associations cautiously.

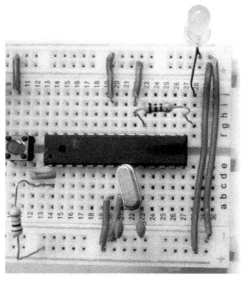

Stage 3:- Now, associate the power supply and microcontroller part utilizing jumpers. Your last circuit will looks something like this.

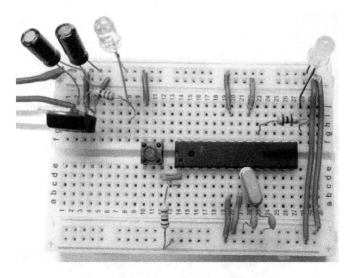

Along these lines, this is our Arduino on breadboard. You can actualize a similar circuit on PCB utilizing basic apparatuses like EasyEDA, and so forth. Presently, we need to transfer the bootloader to the new Atmega 328 IC so we can begin to program the IC.

Part-2: Burning the Bootloader into Atmega328 IC

What is bootloader and why we need it??

Bootloader is little bit of executable code that for all time put away in the microcontroller's memory. This involves under 1Kb of memory. Bootloader enables the IC to acknowledge the code from the PC and spot it in the memory of the microcontroller.

Generally, all the microcontroller from Atmel are customized with the assistance developers which has some extravagant associations. Bootloaders decreases the intricacy and permit us with a simple and productive method for programming the microcontroller. This implies you can program it just by utilizing a USB link.

When you purchase another Atmega 328 from market, it has no bootloader in it. So to program your Atmega328 utilizing Arduino IDE you need to initially transfer the bootloader.

To transfer the Bootloader, we have two strategies:

1. Utilizing USBasp software engineer

2. Utilizing Arduino UNO board

Second strategy is simpler contrasted with initial one. Since it requires less associations and furthermore most recent rendition of Arduino IDE not bolsters the extravagant USBasp software engineers.

Along these lines, in this instructional exercise we will transfer bootloader utilizing Arduino Uno board.

Upload the Arduino Bootloader in Atmega328 Chip

Stage 1:- Open Arduino IDE. Go to File - > Examples - > ArduinoISP. Than pick ArduinoISP. As demonstrated as follows.

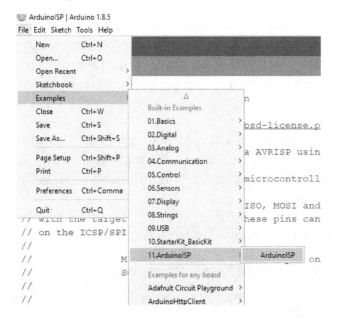

Stage 2:- Now, you need to transfer this code to your Arduino board. Pick the com port and board from the instrument menu and hit the transfer catch.

Stage 3:- After 'Done transferring', separate the Arduino board from the PC and make the associations of Arduino board with Atmega 328 as appeared in underneath chart.

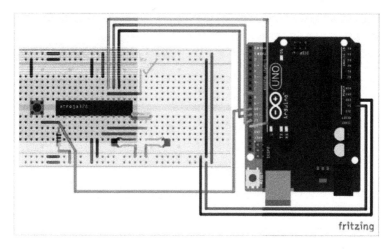

Stage 4:- Now, interface the Arduino board with the PC. Open Arduino IDE.

Go to Tools , Choose board as Arduino/Genuine Uno, Choose the right Port for your board. Pick Programmer as "Arduino as ISP". Try not to mistake it for ArduinoISP. Both are extraordinary.

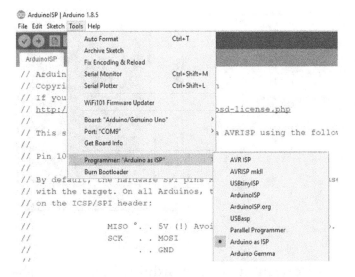

Stage 5:- Now, Go to Tools again and Click on Burn Bootloader just beneath the Programmer choice. Following couple of moments, bootloader is transferred effectively. On the off chance that there is any mistake in transferring, check the associations.

```
// ArduinoISP
// Copyright (c) 2008-2011 Randall Bohn
// If you require a license, see
// http://www.opensource.org/licenses/bsd-license.php
//
// This sketch turns the Arduino into a AVRISP using the following Arduino pins:
//
// Pin 10 is used to reset the target microcontroller.
//
// By default, the hardware SPI pins MISO, MOSI and SCK are used to communicate
// with the target. On all Arduinos, these pins can be found
// on the ICSP/SPI header:
//
//               MISO °. . 5V (!) Avoid this pin on Due, Zero...
//               SCK   . . MOSI
//                     . . GND
//
// On some Arduinos (Uno,...), pins MOSI, MISO and SCK are the same pins as
// digital pin 11, 12 and 13, respectively. That is why many tutorials instruct
// you to hook up the target to these pins. If you find this wiring more
// practical, have a define USE_OLD_STYLE_WIRING. This will work even when not
```

Done burning bootloader

Your breadboard Arduino is prepared to fill in as genuine Arduino board. Presently, question emerges that how to program Atmega 328 IC? That we will talk about in our next area.

Part-3: How to Program Arduino Bootloader uploaded Atmega 328 IC

Independent Arduino Atmega328 Chip can be modified from multiple points of view.

1. Utilizing clear Arduino board for example Arduino board without Atmega 328 IC in it.

2. Utilizing USB to Serial TTL converter module (FTDI module).

3. Utilizing USBasp software engineer (include numerous associations).

Here, we will program it utilizing two strategies: USB to sequential converter and Arduino board.

Programming Atmega328 Chip using Arduino board

Stage 1:- Take an Arduino board without Atmega328 chip. Make the associations of Arduino board with our breadboard Arduino as appeared in this outline.

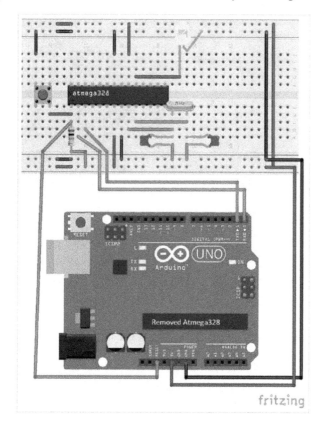

Stage 2:- Connect the Arduino board with the PC as well as open the Arduino IDE. Pick Arduino Uno from Board menu in Tools, Programmer as USBasp and right com port of the board.

Stage 3:- We will begin by transferring the Blink program. So pick the squint program from Examples and hit Upload catch.

Presently, you can see drove on the breadboard will begin flickering.

Programming Arduino Atmega328 Chip using USB to Serial converter

Stage 1:- If you don't have Arduino board. This is the best strategy to program your breadboard Arduino.

Make the connections as:

RXD stick of FTDI - > Tx stick of Atmega328(pin 3)

TXD stick of FTDI - > Rx stick of Atmega328 (stick 2)

GND - > GND(pin 8)

5v - > Vcc (stick 7)

Some FTDI modules has Reset stick otherwise called

DTR stick, which should be associated with the Reset stick of Atmega328 (stick 1). In case there is no reset stick in the module, don't stress I'll give the arrangement when we program the chip.

Stage 2:- Now, associate the FTDI with PC and open Device director in control board. You will see Port area, Expand it. In the event that there is a yellow imprint before the driver, at that point you need to refresh your module driver.

On the off chance that there is no imprint, at that point note the com port number and open Arduino IDE. Go to Tools - > Ports - > Select the com that you have noted.

Stage 3:- Now, We will transfer flicker program to our Breadboard Arduino. Go to File - > Examples - > Basics - > Blink. Pick Arduino Uno from Board menu in apparatuses, Programmer as USBasp and right com port of the board.

At that point hit transfer catch.

Note: If your FTDI module has no DTR stick, at that point Press the Reset catch on the breadboard and hit transfer catch. Keep it squeezed in the event that it says Compiling sketch... Release the catch when it says Uploading...

Presently, the program will be effectively transferred into Arduino Bootloader Atmega328 chip.

6.THERMAL PRINTER INTERFACING WITH ARDUINO UNO

You simply made installment to an eatery and got a little bill or apportioned money from an ATM and got the exchange receipt. These receipts are printed utilizing a Thermal printer or receipt printer.

Warm printer is the promptly accessible and financially savvy answer for print little bills or receipts. This simple to incorporate arrangement is accessible all over. The printer utilizes thermochromic paper, a unique kind of paper which changes into dark shading when it is presented to a specific measure of warmth. Warm printer utilizes a unique warming procedure to print on this paper. The printer head is warmed in an exceptional electrical to keep up a specific temperature. At the point when the warm paper goes through its head, its warm covering transforms into dark where the head is warmed.

In the past venture, we have interfaced Thermal printer with PIC Microcontroller. In this instructional exercise, we will interface a warm printer with the Arduino Uno board. This undertaking will work this way:-

1. The printer will be associated with Arduino Uno.

2. A material switch is being associated with the Arduino board to give the 'push to print' alternative when squeezed.

3. Locally available Arduino LED will tell the printing status. It will sparkle just when the printing action is going on.

Printer Specification and connections

We are utilizing CSN A1 Thermal Printer from Cashino, which is accessible effectively and the cost isn't excessively high.

On the off chance that we see the determination on its official site, we will see a table which gives the definite particulars

Specification:

Print	Printing Method	Thermal Line
	Printing Speed	50-80mm/s
	Resolution	8 dots/mm, 384 dots/line
	Effective Printing Width	48mm
Character	Character Set	ASCII,GB2312-80(Chinese)
	Print Font	ANK:(8x16,9x17,9x24,12×24), GBK: 16×16,24×24
Paper Spec	Paper Type	Thermal paper
	Paper Width	57.5± 0.5mm
	Paper Roll Diameter	Max: 40mm
Reliability	MCBF	5 million lines
Interface		Serial(RS-232,TTL),USB
Insert Depth		34.65mm
Power Supply (Adapter)		DC5V-9V/12V
Physical	Outline Dimension (WxDxH)	76.8x77.4x47.7mm
	Installation Port Size	72.8 x 73.26mm
	Color	Beige/Black(can be customized)
Environment	Operating Temp	5°C ~ 50°C
	Operating Humidity	10% ~ 80%
	Storage Temp	-20°C ~ 60°C
	Storage Humidity	10% ~ 90%

On the rear of the printer, we will see the accompanying association

The TTL connector gives the Rx Tx association with speak with the microcontroller unit. We can likewise utilize the RS232 convention to speak with the printer. The power connector is for driving the printer and the catch is utilized for printer testing reason. At the point when the printer is being controlled, in the event that we push the individual test catch the printer, will print a sheet where details and test lines will be printed. Here is the individual test sheet-

As should be obvious the printer utilize 9600 baud rate to speak with the microcontroller unit. The printer can print ASCII characters. The correspondence is extremely simple, we can print anything by essentially utilizing UART, transmitting string or character.

The printer works from 5-9V, we will utilize a 9V 2A power supply which can control both the printer and the Arduino Uno. The printer needs more than 1.5A of current for warming the printer head. This is the disadvantage of the warm printer as it takes colossal burden current during the printing procedure.

Prerequisites

To make the accompanying undertaking, we need the accompanying things:-

1. Breadboard
2. Hook up wires
3. Arduino UNO board with USB Cable.
4. A computer with Arduino interface setup ready with the Arduino IDE.
5. 10k resistor
6. Tactile switch
7. Warm Printer CSN A1 with paper roll
8. 9V 2A appraised power supply unit.

Circuit Diagram and Explanation

Schematic for controlling printer with Arduino Uno is given beneath:

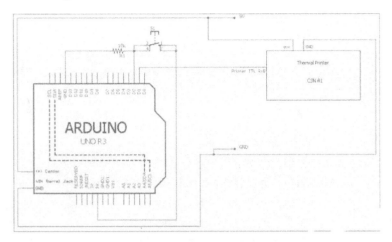

The circuit is basic. We are utilizing a resistor to give default state over the Switch info stick D2. At the point when the catch is squeezed, D2 will turn out to be HIGH and this condition is utilized to trigger the printing. Single power supply of 9V 2A power supply is utilized to control the warm printer and Arduino board. It is critical to check the power supply extremity before interfacing it to the Arduino UNO board. It has a barrel jack contribution with focus positive extremity.

We developed the circuit in a breadboard and tried it.

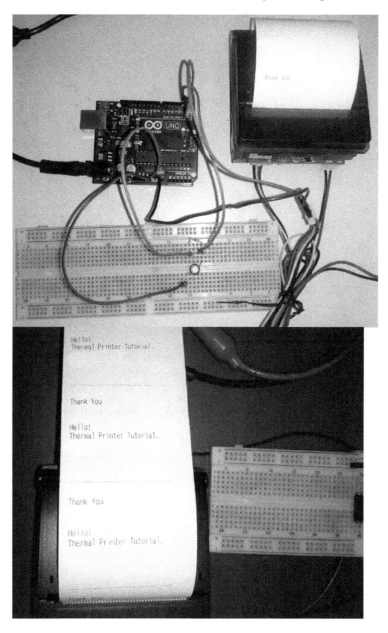

Arduino Program

From the outset, we pronounced the pins for push-button (Pin 2) and on board LED (Pin13)

```
int led = 13;

int SW = 2;
```

At that point couple of factors are arranged for de-bounce deferral and switch press status

```
int is_switch_press = 0; // For detecting the switch press status

int debounce_delay = 300; //Debounce delay
```

In the arrangement work, we designed the LED stick as yield and switch as info. We likewise arranged the UART with 9600 baud rate.

```
void setup() {

/*
```

```
 *  This function is used to set the pin configuration

 */

 pinMode(led, OUTPUT);

 pinMode(SW, INPUT);

 Serial.begin(9600);

}
```

In the primary circle, we first check whether the switch is squeezed or not, at the same time we hang tight for at some point and again check to distinguish that the switch is really squeezed or not, if the switch is as yet squeezed even after the postponement, we print custom lines in the UART, so in the Thermal printer.

Toward the beginning of printing we set the installed LED high and in the wake of printing, we turned it off by making it low.

```
void loop() {

 is_switch_press = digitalRead(SW); // Reading
the Switch press status
```

```
 if (is_switch_press == HIGH){

   delay(debounce_delay); // debounce delay for
 button press

   if(is_switch_press == HIGH){

   digitalWrite(led, HIGH);

   Serial.println("Hello");

   delay(100);

   Serial.println("This is a Thermal printer inter-
 face");

   Serial.println("with Arduino UNO.");

   delay(100);

   Serial.println("hellow.com");

   Serial.println ("\n\r");

   Serial.println ("\n\r");

   Serial.println ("\n\r");

   Serial.println ("---------------------------- \n \r");
```

```
Serial.println ("Thank You.");

Serial.println ("\n\r");

Serial.println ("\n\r");

Serial.println ("\n\r");

digitalWrite(led, LOW);

}

}

else{

digitalWrite(led, LOW);

}

}
```

Check the total Arduino code beneath.
Code
```
/*
 * This code is to use in Arduino UNO for interfacing
the Thermal Printer.

*/
//Pin declaration
```

```
int led = 13;
int SW = 2;
// Programe flow related operations
int is_switch_press = 0; // For detecting the switch
press status
int debounce_delay = 300; //Debounce delay
void setup() {
/*
*  This function is used to set the pin configuration
*/
pinMode(led, OUTPUT);
pinMode(SW, INPUT);
Serial.begin(9600);
}
void loop() {
  is_switch_press = digitalRead(SW); // Reading the
Switch press status
 if(is_switch_press == HIGH){
   delay(debounce_delay); // debounce delay for but-
ton press
  if(is_switch_press == HIGH){
  digitalWrite(led, HIGH);
  Serial.println("Hello");
  delay(100);
  Serial.println("This is a Thermal printer interface");
  Serial.println("with Arduino UNO.");
  delay(100);
  Serial.println("Hello.com");
  Serial.println ("\n\r");
  Serial.println ("\n\r");
```

```
Serial.println ("\n\r");
Serial.println ("---------------------------- \n \r");
Serial.println ("Thank You.");
Serial.println ("\n\r");
Serial.println ("\n\r");
Serial.println ("\n\r");
digitalWrite(led, LOW);
}
}
else{
digitalWrite(led, LOW);
}
}
```

7.DIGITAL COMPASS USING ARDUINO AND HMC5883L MAGNETOMETER

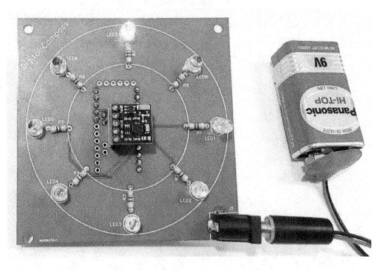

Human cerebrum is worked of complex layer of

structures which encourages us to be a prevailing animal categories on earth. For instance the entorhinal cortex in your cerebrum can provide you feeling of guidance helping you to explore effectively through spots that you are curious about. In any case, in contrast to us, Robots and unmanned Ariel vehicles need something to get this ability to know east from west so they could move self-rulingly in new territories and scenes. Various robots utilize various sorts of sensors to achieve this, yet the regularly utilized one is a magnetometer, which could advise the robot where geo-realistic bearing it is as of now looking at. This won't just assist the robot with sensing bearing yet additionally to alternate in a pre-characterized heading and holy messenger.

Since the sensor could show the geo-realistic North, South, East and West, we people could likewise utilize it on occasion when required. In this article let us attempt to see how Magnetometer sensor functions and how to interface it with a microcontroller like Arduino. Here we will construct a cool Digital Compass which will help us in finding the bearings by shining a LED pointing North Direction. This Digital Compass is perfectly created on PCB from PCBGOGO, with the goal that I can convey it next time when I go out in the wild and wish that I would get lost just to utilize this thing for finding back the way home. We should begin.

Materials Required

1. HMC5883L Magnetometer sensor
2. Arduino Pro mini
3. 47Ohm Resistor – 8Nos
4. LED lights - 8Nos
5. A solid PCB producer like PCBgogo
6. Barrel Jack
7. PC/Laptop
8. FTDI Programmer for mini

What is a Magnetometer and How does it Work?

Before we plunge into the circuit, we should comprehend somewhat about magnetometer and how they work. As the name proposes the term Magneto does not allude to that insane freak in wonder who could control metals by simply playing piano noticeable all around. Ohh! In any case, I like that person he is cool.

Magnetometer is really a bit of gear that could detect the attractive shafts of the earth and point the bearing as indicated by that. We as a whole realize that Earth is colossal bit of circular magnet with North Pole and South Pole. Also, there is attractive field due to it. A Magnetometer detects this attractive field as well as dependent on the course of the attractive field it can identify the heading we are confronting.

How the HMC5883L Sensor Module Works

The HMC5883L being a magnetometer sensor does likewise. It has the HMC5883L IC on it which is from Honeywell. This IC has 3 magneto-resistive materials inside which are orchestrated in the tomahawks x, y and z. The measure of current moving through these materials is touchy to the world's attractive field. So by estimating the adjustment in current coursing through these materials we can identify the adjustment in Earth's attractive field. When the change is attractive field is assimilated the qualities would then be able to be sent to any inserted controller like a microcontroller or processor through the I2C convention.

Since the sensor works by detecting the attractive field, the yield esteems will be extraordinarily influenced if a metal is set close-by. This conduct can be utilized to utilize these sensors as metal locators too. Care ought to be taken not to bring magnets close to this sensor since the solid attractive field from a magnet may trigger false qualities on the sensor.

Difference between HMC5883L and QMC5883L

There is a typical disarray spinning around these sensors for some novices. This is on the grounds that a few merchants (in reality most) sell the QMC5883L sensors rather than the first HMC5883L from Honeywell. The most part in light of the fact that the QMC5883L is route less expensive than the HMC5883L module. The tragic part is that the working of these two sensors is somewhat extraordinary and a similar code can't be utilized for both. This is on the grounds that the I2C address of both the sensors isn't the equivalent. The code give in this instructional exercise will work just for QMC5883L the regularly accessible sensor module.

To realize which model of sensor you are having, you simply need to look up carefully at the IC itself to peruse what is composed over it. In the event that it is composed something like L883, at that point it is the HMC58836L and on the off chance that it is composed something like DA5883, at that point it is the QMC5883L IC. Both the modules are appeared in picture beneath for simple downplaying.

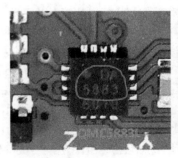

Circuit Diagram

The circuit for this Arduino based Digital Compass is entirely basic, we just need to interface the HM-C5883L sensor with the Arduino and associate 8 LEDs to the GPIO pins of the Arduino Pro smaller than expected. The total circuit graph is demonstrated as follows

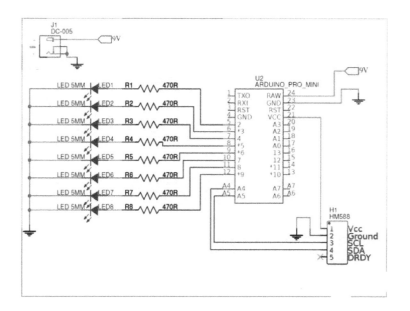

The Sensor module has 5 sticks out of which the DRDY (Data Ready) isn't utilized in our task since we are working the sensor in nonstop mode. The Vcc as well as ground stick is utilized to control the Module with 5V from the Arduino board. The SCL and SDA are the I2C correspondence transport lines that are associated with the A4 and A5 I2C pins of the Arduino Pro smaller than normal separately. Since the module itself has a force high resistor on the lines, there is no compelling reason to include them remotely.

To demonstrate the bearing we have utilized 8 LEDs which are all associated with the GPIO pins of the Arduino through a present restricting resistor of 470 Ohms. The Complete circuit is controlled by a 9V battery through the barrel Jack. This 9V is given legitimately to the Vin stick of the Arduino where it is managed to 5V utilizing the on-board controller on Arduino. This 5V is then used to control the sensor and the Arduino also.

Fabricating the PCBs for the Digital Compass

The possibility of the circuit is place the 8 LEDs in a roundabout manner with the goal that each Led focuses all the 8 headings to be specific North, North-East, East, South-East, South, South-West, West and North West separately. So it is difficult to orchestrate them perfectly on a breadboard or even on a perf board besides. Building up a PCB for this circuit will make it look progressively flawless and simple to utilize. So I opened my PCB planning programming and put the LEDs and resistor in a perfect round example and associated the tracks to frame the associations. My Design looked something like this underneath when finished. You can likewise download the Gerber record from the connection given beneath.

- Download Gerber document for Digital Compass PCB

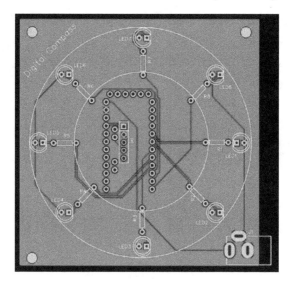

I have planned it to be a twofold side board since I need the Arduino to be in the base side of my PCB with the goal that it doesn't ruin the look over my PCB. In case you are stressing that you need to pay high for a twofold side PCB then hang on I got great new coming.

Presently, that our Design is prepared the time has come to get them manufactured. To complete the PCB is very simple, essentially pursue the means underneath

Stage 1: Get into www.pcbgogo.com, join if this is your first time. At that point, in the PCB Prototype tab enter the components of your PCB, the quantity of layers and the quantity of PCB you require. My PCB is 80cm×80cm so the tab resembles this underneath

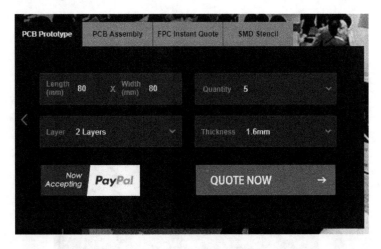

Stage 2: Proceed by tapping on the Quote Now catch. You will be taken to a page where to set couple of extra parameters whenever required like the material utilized track separating and so on. Be that as it may, for the most part the default esteems will work fine. The main is we need to consider here is the cost and time. As should be obvious the Build Time is just 2-3 days and it just costs $5 for our PSB. You would then be able to choose a favored dispatching strategy dependent on your prerequisite.

Stage 3: The last advance is to transfer the Gerber record and continue with the installment. To ensure the procedure is smooth PCBGOGO confirms if your Gerber document is legitimate before continuing with the installment. In this direction you can sure that your PCB is creation well disposed and will contact you as submitted.

Assembling the PCB

After the board was requested, it contacted me after certain days however messenger in a conveniently marked all around pressed box and like consistently the nature of the PCB was amazing. I am sharing couple of photos of the sheets underneath for you to pass judgment.

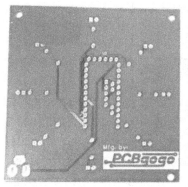 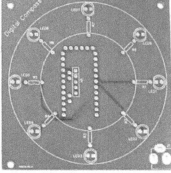

I turned on my binding pole and began gathering the Board. Since the Footprints, cushions, vias and silkscreen are flawlessly of the correct shape and size I had no issue collecting the board. The load up was prepared in only a little ways from the hour of unloading the container.

Scarcely any photos of the board in the wake of welding are demonstrated as follows.

Programming the Arduino

Since our equipment is prepared, given us a chance to investigate the program that must be transferred into our Arduino board. The reason for the code is to peruse the information from the QMC5883L magnetometer sensor and convert it into degree (0 to 360). When we know the degree, we need to turn on a the LED pointing a particular bearing. The heading I have utilized in this program is north. So independent of where you are there might be one LED shining on your board and the bearing of the LED will show the NORTH course. Once could later figure the other bearing is one heading is known.

The total code for this Digital Compass Project can be found toward the part of the bargain. You can legitimately transfer it on your board subsequent to including the library and you are prepared to go. However, on the off chance that you must know more on what is really occurring in the code read further.

As told before we are utilizing the QMC5883L IC, to speak with the IC we have to realize the I2C address of its registers which can be found in its datasheet. In any case, fortunate for every one of us of that is as of now done and is bundled as a library by a person called keepworking on Github. So you should simply essentially download the Library for QMC5883L by tapping on the connection to get a ZIP document. This ZIP record would then be able to be included into your Arduino IDE by following Sketch - > Include Library - > Add .ZIP library.

After the Library is included, we can continue with our program. We start the program by including the required library documents as demonstrated as follows. The wire library is utilized to empower I2C correspondence and the MechaQMC5883 is the one that we just added to Arduino. This library holds all the data on the best way to converse with the EMC5883L sensor.

```
#include <Wire.h> //Wire Librarey for I2C com-
```

munication

```
#include <MechaQMC5883.h> //QMC5883 Li-
brarey is added since mine is QMC583 and not
HMC5883
```

In the following line, we make an article name for the sensor we are utilizing. I have utilized the name qmc yet it very well may be anything you like.

```
MechaQMC5883 qmc; //Create an object name for
the snsor, I have named it as qmc
```

Next, we get into the worldwide variable presentations. Here since we have 8 Led as yields, it is difficult to allude to every one through stick name, so we are utilizing the cluster choice to allude to every one of the LEDs. The name of the cluster is ledPins and the variable led_count is the quantity of driven we have. It begins with 0.

```
int ledPins[] = {2,3,4,5,6,7,8,9}; //Array of output
pin to which the LED is connected to

char led_count = 7; //Total number of LED pins
```

Inside the void arrangement work, we instate the I2C correspondence, Serial correspondence and the sensor too. At that point we announce all the LED sticks as yield pins. Since we have utilized an exhibit, it is anything but difficult to allude to every one of the pins by utilizing a for circle and exploring through the for circle as demonstrated as follows.

```
void setup() {

  Wire.begin(); //Begin I2C communication

  Serial.begin(9600); //Begin Serial Communication

  qmc.init(); //Initialise the QMC5883 Sensor

  for (int thisPin=0; thisPin <= led_count; thisPin++){ //Navigate through all the pins in array

    pinMode(ledPins[thisPin],OUTPUT); //Declare them as output

  }

}
```

In the fundamental circle which is an unending one, we need to get the estimations of x,y and z from the sensor and figure the degree the sensor is presently confronting. To peruse the estimations of x,y and z utilize the accompanying line

```
int x,y,z;

qmc.read(&x,&y,&z); //Get the values of X,Y and Z
from sensor
```

The formulae to ascertain the heading in degree is demonstrated as follows. Since we are not going to turn the compass along the z hub we don't consider that esteem. This formulae can be utilized just if the IC level surface is looking up like it is in our set-up. When heading is determined, the worth will be in range - 180 to 180 which we need to change over to 0 to 360 like we would discover in every single advanced compass.

```
int heading=atan2(x, y)/0.0174532925; //Calcu-
late the degree using X and Y parameters with this
formulae

//Convert result into 0 to 360

  if(heading < 0)

  heading+=360;

  heading = 360-heading;
```

The last advance is to sparkle the LED pointing in the NORTH course. To do that we have arrangement of if conditions explanations where we check in what range the degree is presently in and turn on the LED by that. The code is appear beneath

```
//Based on the value of heading print the result for debugging and glow the respective LED.

 if (heading > 338 || heading < 22)

 {

   Serial.println("NORTH");

   digitalWrite(ledPins[0],HIGH);

 }

 if (heading > 22 && heading < 68)

 {

   Serial.println("NORTH-EAST");

   digitalWrite(ledPins[7],HIGH);

 }
```

```
if (heading > 68 && heading < 113)

{

  Serial.println("EAST");

  digitalWrite(ledPins[6],HIGH);

}

if (heading > 113 && heading < 158)

{

  Serial.println("SOUTH-EAST");

  digitalWrite(ledPins[5],HIGH);

}

if (heading > 158 && heading < 203)

{

  Serial.println("SOUTH");

  digitalWrite(ledPins[4],HIGH);

}
```

```
if (heading > 203 && heading < 248)

{

  Serial.println("SOTUH-WEST");

  digitalWrite(ledPins[3],HIGH);

}

if (heading > 248 && heading < 293)

{

  Serial.println("WEST");

  digitalWrite(ledPins[2],HIGH);

}

if (heading > 293 && heading < 338)

{

  Serial.println("NORTH-WEST");

  digitalWrite(ledPins[1],HIGH);

}
```

The rationale behind the code esteems can be comprehended by taking a gander at the table underneath. Essentially we ascertain which course we are confronting and anticipate the north bearing and gleam the individual LED.

Direction	Degree corresponding to Direction	Range for that Direction
NORTH	0° / 360°	>338° or < 22°
NORTH-EAST	45°	22° to 68°
EAST	90°	68° to 113°
SOTUH-EAST	135°	113° to 158°
SOUTH	180°	158° to 203°
SOUTH-WEST	225°	203° to 248°
WEST	170°	248° to 293°
NORTH-WEST	315°	293° to 338°

The last part of the program is to set how quick the outcome must be refreshed. I have make a deferral for 500 milli seconds and after that made all the LED to mood killer to begin again frame the first inside the void circle. Be that as it may, in case you need quicker refreshes you can diminish the postpone further down.

```
delay(500); // update position of LED for every alf seconds
```

```
//Turn off the all the LED

  for (int thisPin=0; thisPin <= led_count; thisPin
++){

  digitalWrite(ledPins[thisPin],LOW);

}
```

Testing the Digital Compass

Since we have utilized the Arduino master smaller than normal we need an outer developer like a FTDI board to transfer the program. When the program is transferred, you should see one LED is shining on the board, the bearing where the LED is gleaming will be the NORTH heading.

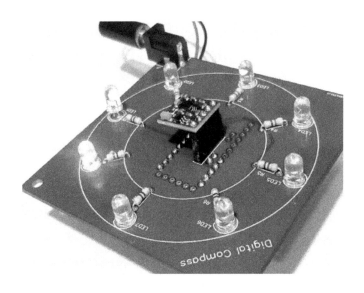

You would then be able to play with the Board by pivoting it and check if the LED still indicates the north course. You can utilize a 9V battery whenever to control the set-up and check the bearing you are confronting. You may take note of that the qualities will get off-base when there is a substantial metal piece close to your board or regardless of whether you pivot the board along the Z hub. There are approaches to conquer this issue and that is for another instructional exercise.

Expectation you have delighted in the instructional exercise and picked up something valuable out of it. In the event that truly, at that point the credits go to PCBGOGO who have supported this post, so try them out for your PCB's.

Code

```
/*
 * Program for Arduino Digital Compass using
QMC5883

 * Lib. from https://github.com/keepworking/
Mecha_QMC5883L
 * WARNING: This code works only for QMC5883 Sen-
sor which is commonly being sold as HMC5883 read
article to find the actual name of the sensor you have.
 */
#include <Wire.h> //Wire Librarey for I2C communi-
```

cation

```
#include <MechaQMC5883.h> //QMC5883 Librarey
is added since mine is QMC583 and not HMC5883

MechaQMC5883 qmc; //Create an object name for the
snsor, I have named it as qmc

int ledPins[] = {2,3,4,5,6,7,8,9}; //Array of output pin
to which the LED is connected to

char led_count = 7; //Total number of LED pins


void setup() {
 Wire.begin(); //Begin I2C communication
 Serial.begin(9600); //Begin Serial Communication
 qmc.init(); //Initialise the QMC5883 Sensor
  for (int thisPin=0; thisPin <= led_count; thisPin++)
{ //Navigate through all the pins in array
     pinMode(ledPins[thisPin],OUTPUT);  //Declare
them as output
 }
}
void loop() { //Infinite Loop
 int x,y,z;
  qmc.read(&x,&y,&z); //Get the values of X,Y and Z
from sensor


  int heading=atan2(x, y)/0.0174532925; //Calculate
the degree using X and Y parameters with this formu-
lae
 //Convert result into 0 to 360
```

```
if(heading < 0)
heading+=360;
heading = 360-heading;


  Serial.println(heading); //Print the value of heading
in degree for debugging
//Based on the value of heading print the result for de-
bugging and glow the respective LED.
 if(heading > 338 || heading < 22)
 {
 Serial.println("NORTH");
 digitalWrite(ledPins[0],HIGH);
 }
 if(heading > 22 && heading < 68)
 {
 Serial.println("NORTH-EAST");
 digitalWrite(ledPins[7],HIGH);
 }
 if(heading > 68 && heading < 113)
 {
 Serial.println("EAST");
 digitalWrite(ledPins[6],HIGH);
 }
 if(heading > 113 && heading < 158)
 {
 Serial.println("SOUTH-EAST");
 digitalWrite(ledPins[5],HIGH);
 }
 if(heading > 158 && heading < 203)
 {
```

```
  Serial.println("SOUTH");
  digitalWrite(ledPins[4],HIGH);
  }
  if(heading > 203 && heading < 248)
  {
  Serial.println("SOTUH-WEST");
  digitalWrite(ledPins[3],HIGH);
  }
  if(heading > 248 && heading < 293)
  {
  Serial.println("WEST");
  digitalWrite(ledPins[2],HIGH);
  }
  if(heading > 293 && heading < 338)
  {
  Serial.println("NORTH-WEST");
  digitalWrite(ledPins[1],HIGH);
  }
  delay(500); // update position of LED for every alf
seconds
//Turn off the all the LED
  for (int thisPin=0; thisPin <= led_count; thisPin++){
  digitalWrite(ledPins[thisPin],LOW);
  }
  }
```

8.HOW TO PLOT REAL TIME TEMPERATURE GRAPH USING MATLAB

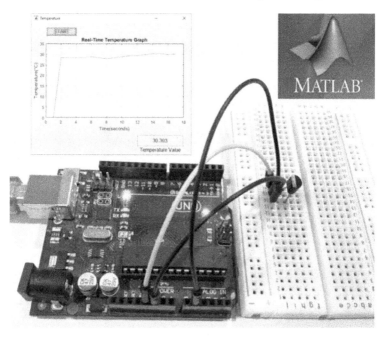

Charts are constantly useful to picture the information and it turns out to be exceptionally simple to discover patterns and examples by taking a gander at them. There are numerous product accessible to plot diagrams dependent on the info esteems, today we will utilize MATLAB to plot chart dependent on the temperature information from LM35 sensor. This instructional exercise will give you an essential thought regarding how to plot ongoing chart utilizing MATLAB. Arduino Uno is utilized here to get temperature information from LM35 temperature sensor.

Prior to continuing further, on the off chance that

you are new to MATLAB you can check our past MAT-LAB instructional exercises for better downplaying:

- Beginning with MATLAB: A Quick Introduction

- Interfacing Arduino with MATLAB - Blinking LED

- Sequential Communication among MATLAB and Arduino

- DC Motor Control Using MATLAB and Arduino

- Stepper Motor Control utilizing MATLAB and Arduino

Creating MATLAB Graphical User Interface for Plotting Graph

First we need to construct GUI (Graphical User Interface) for Plot a Graph with the temperature information. To dispatch the GUI, type the beneath direction in the order window

```
guide
```

A popup window will open, at that point select new clear GUI as appeared in underneath picture,

Presently we need to pick one push catch, two toma-hawks and one content box for MATLAB graphical interface. Push catch will be utilized for beginning the temperature detecting, two tomahawks for plot-ting the chart and Text box to demonstrate the pre-sent estimation of temperature.

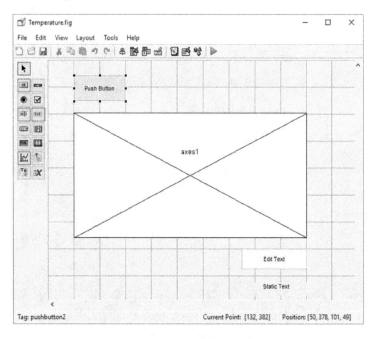

To resize or to change the state of the catch, Axes or alter content catch, simply click on it and you will probably drag the sides of the catch. By double tapping on any of these you will probably change the shading, string and tag of that specific catch. After customization it will resemble this

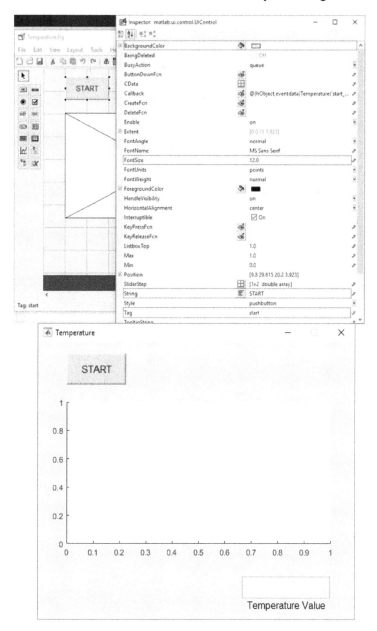

You can change the catches according to your decision. Presently when you spare this, a code is produced in the Editor window of MATLAB. To make your Arduino to play out a specific assignment identified with your task, you generally need to alter this produced code. So underneath we have altered the MATLAB code. You can become well-known with Command window, supervisor window and so on in Getting started with MATLAB instructional exercise.

MATLAB Code for Plotting the Graph

Complete MATLAB code for Designing a Thermometer utilizing LM35 and Arduino, is given toward the part of the bargain. Further we are including the GUI document (.fig) and code file(.m) here for download, utilizing which you can alter the catches or Axes size according to your necessity. We have altered the created code as clarified beneath.

Reorder the underneath code on line no. 74 to ensure that the Arduino is chatting with MATLAB each time you run the m-document.

```
clear all;

global a;

a = arduino();
```

```
71
72    % Get default command line output from handles structure
73 -   varargout{1} = handles.output;
74 -   clear all;
75 -   global a;
76 -   a = arduino();
```

When you look down, you will see that there are two capacities made for Pushbutton and Edit Text in the GUI, no capacity will be made for Axes. Presently compose the code in the Pushbutton (start catch) work as per the errand you need to perform.

In Start catch's capacity, reorder the underneath code just before the completion of the capacity to begin the temperature detecting. For consistently detecting, showing and graphical plotting of the temperature, we are utilizing while circle. We have given respite of 1 second after each emphasis so temperature worth will be refreshed each second.

```
x = 0;

go = true;

global a;

while go

value = readVoltage(a,'A1');

temp = (value*100);
```

```
disp(temp);

x = [x temp];

plot(handles.axes1,x);

grid on;

xlabel('Time(seconds)')

ylabel('Temperature(°C)');

title('Real-Time Temperature Graph');

drawnow

set(handles.edit1,'String',num2str(temp));

pause(1);

end
```

```
78      % --- Executes on button press in start.
79    □ function start_Callback(hObject, eventdata, handles)
80    □ % hObject    handle to start (see GCBO)
81      % eventdata  reserved - to be defined in a future version of MATLAB
82    ┤ % handles    structure with handles and user data (see GUIDATA)
83 -    x = 0;
84 -    go = true;
85 -    global a;
86 -  □ while go
87
88 -    value = readVoltage(a,'A1');
89 -    temp = (value*100);
90 -    disp(temp);
91 -    x = [x temp];
92 -    plot(handles.axes1,x);
93 -    grid on;
94 -    xlabel('Time(seconds)')
95 -    ylabel('Temperature(°C)');
96 -    title('Real-Time Temperature Graph');
97 -    drawnow
98 -    set(handles.edit1,'String',num2str(temp));
99 -    pause(1);
100 -   └ end
```

Presently, lets perceive how the code is functioning. In beneath three lines line we have set the underlying estimation of 'x' to zero, characterizing 'go' as consistent with beginning the while circle and pronounced 'worldwide a' for calling the Arduino in the capacity.

```
x = 0;

go = true;

global a;
```

Underneath line of code is utilized to detect the voltage esteem from the simple stick A1 of the Arduino which is associated with the 'OUT' stick of the LM35

Temperature Sensor. The yield will be the voltage esteem not the simple worth.

```
value = readVoltage(a,'A1');
```

Here we can legitimately change over the voltage esteem into the temperature esteem (degree Celsius), by increasing it by 10

```
temp = (value*100);
```

Presently, to plot the diagram 'plot(handles.axes1,x)' work is utilized, where axes1 is the reference or name of the Graph zone. So in the event that you are plotting more than one chart, at that point you simply have to change the name of the tomahawks, as on the off chance that you plot another diagram you can compose plot(handles.axes2,x)'

'Framework on' is utilized to On the Grid perspective on the diagram, 'xlabel', 'ylabel' and 'title' are utilized for naming the x-hub, y-hub and title.

```
plot(handles.axes1,x);

grid on;
```

```
xlabel('Time(seconds)')

ylabel('Temperature(°C)');

title('Real-Time Temperature Graph');
```

'Drawnow' is utilized to refresh the graphical portrayal progressively.

```
drawnow
```

To show the estimation of the temperature in the alter content box at consistently underneath direction is utilized,

```
set(handles.edit1,'String',num2str(temp));
```

Material Required

1. Breadboard
2. Arduino UNO
3. MATLAB introduced Laptop (Preference: R2016a or above forms)
4. Connecting Wires
5. LM35 - Temperature Sensor

Circuit Diagram

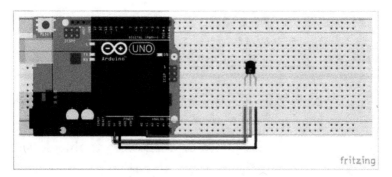

Plot the Graph with MATLAB

Subsequent to setting the equipment as indicated by circuit chart, simply click on the run catch to run the altered code in .m document

MATLAB may take few moments to react, don't tap on any GUI catches until MATLAB is indicating occupied message in the lower left corner as demonstrated as follows,

When everything is prepared, click on the beginning catch and you will begin getting the temperature information on the Graphical Area and in the Edit Text box. The worth will naturally refresh in each one second. This interim of one second you can change in the MATLAB code as needs be.

The yield will resemble the picture demonstrated as follows,

This is the way you can plot the chart for any approaching an incentive from the Arduino utilizing MATLAB.

Code

MATLAB Code:

```
function varargout = Temperature(varargin)
gui_Singleton = 1;
gui_State = struct('gui_Name',   mfilename, ...
        'gui_Singleton', gui_Singleton, ...
            'gui_OpeningFcn', @Temperature_Open-
ingFcn, ...
        'gui_OutputFcn', @Temperature_OutputFcn, ...
        'gui_LayoutFcn', [], ...
        'gui_Callback',  []);
if nargin && ischar(varargin{1})
  gui_State.gui_Callback = str2func(varargin{1});
end
if nargout
    [varargout{1:nargout}] = gui_mainfcn(gui_State,
varargin{:});
else
  gui_mainfcn(gui_State, varargin{:});
end
function Temperature_OpeningFcn(hObject, event-
data, handles, varargin)
handles.output = hObject;
guidata(hObject, handles);
function varargout = Temperature_OutputFcn(hOb-
ject, eventdata, handles)
```

```
varargout{1} = handles.output;
clear all;
global a;
a = arduino;
function start_Callback(hObject, eventdata, handles)
x = 0;
go = true;
global a;
while go


value = readVoltage(a,'A1');
temp = (value*100);
disp(temp);
x = [x temp];
plot(handles.axes1,x);
grid on;
xlabel('Time(seconds)')
ylabel('Temperature(°C)');
title('Real-Time Temperature Graph');
drawnow
set(handles.edit1,'String',num2str(temp));
pause(1);
end

function edit1_Callback(hObject, eventdata, han-
dles)

function edit1_CreateFcn(hObject, eventdata, han-
dles)

if ispc && isequal(get(hObject,'BackgroundColor'),
get(0,'defaultUicontrolBackgroundColor'))
```

```
  set(hObject,'BackgroundColor','white');
end
```

9.SERIAL COMMUNICATION BETWEEN MATLAB AND ARDUINO

MATLAB is flexible programming and can be used for wide assortment of uses. In past instructional exercises of MATLAB, we have disclosed how to utilize MATLAB to control DC engine, Servo engine and Home machines. Here in this instructional exercise, we will find out how to utilize MATLAB for Serial Communication. For the less than desirable part of the arrangement, we are here utilizing Arduino.

There are two different ways to arrangement sequential correspondence among MATLAB and Arduino, one is utilizing order window and other is utilizing MATLAB GUI. The Arduino code for both the strategies will continue as before. In case you are new to

MATLAB, at that point it is prescribe to begin with basic LED flicker program with MATLAB and gain proficiency with the fundamental wording utilized in MATLAB.

Components Required

1. Arduino UNO
2. MATLAB introduced Laptop (Preference: R2016a or above renditions)
3. Resistor (330 ohm)
4. LED (any color)

Circuit Diagram

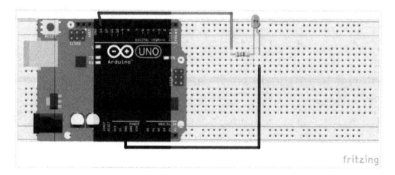

The above circuit graph will stay same for both the approaches to set up sequential correspondence among MATLAB and Arduino.

Serial Communication using MATLAB Command Window

This is the basic technique to arrangement sequential correspondence among Arduino and MATLAB. Here we will just send the information from MATLAB to the Arduino sequentially utilizing direction window and afterward Arduino read the approaching sequential information. At that point this sequentially transmitted information can be utilized to control anything associated with the Arduino. Here we have associated a LED to Arduino, that will be turned on and off as per the sequentially gotten information by the Arduino.

To start with, transfer the given Arduino code in the Arduino UNO as well as after that start coding in MATLAB Editor Window. To open another proofreader content snap on 'New Script' as appeared in underneath picture:

At that point, reorder the beneath complete MATLAB code in the editorial manager window for sequential correspondence among MATLAB and Arduino.

```
%MATLAB Code for Serial Communication be-
tween Arduino and MATLAB

x=serial('COM18','BAUD', 9600);

fopen(x);

go = true;

while go

a= input('Press 1 to turn ON LED & 0 to turn OFF:');

fprintf(x,a);
```

```
if (a == 2)

  go=false;

end

end
```

```
1 -    x=serial('COM18','BAUD', 9600);
2 -    fopen(x);
3
4 -  ⊟ for m=1:inf
5
6 -    a= input('Press 1 to turn ON LED and 0 to t:');
7
8 -    fprintf(x,a);
9 -    if (a == 2)
10 -       break
11 -   end
12 -  ⌐ end
```

In the given code, underneath order is utilized for characterizing the sequential correspondence in MATLAB. Ensure the com port number is the port number on which Arduino is associated and the baud rate ought to be set same in the both the codes of Arduino and MATLAB.

```
x=serial('COM18','BAUD', 9600);
```

To open sequential port utilize the underneath order,

```
fopen(x);
```

Beneath order is utilized to send information from MATLAB to Arduino sequentially, where x is for calling sequential and an is the worth entered by the client.

```
fprintf(x,a);
```

We have use while work for making an unbounded circle and at whatever point the client input the number '2' the circle will break.

```
while go

a= input('Press 1 to turn ON LED & 0 to turn OFF:');

fprintf(x,a);

if (a == 2)

  go=false;

end

end
```

Subsequent to finishing coding the MATLAB editorial manager content snap on 'RUN' to run your program as appeared in beneath picture,

MATLAB takes few moments for preparing the code and start the sequential correspondence, hold up until MATLAB demonstrates 'Occupied' message at the base left corner of the product screen, as appeared in beneath picture.

Presently, you will see the order window for sending the client input, we have set the default message,

'Press 1 to turn ON LED & 0 to turn OFF:'

Send '1' to turn on the LED, '0' to mood killer the LED and '2' to break the activity. You can set any number for any errand, you should simply change the Arduino code appropriately. Whole Arduino program is given toward the end.

```
Command Window
    >> Untitled4
    Press 1 to turn ON LED & 0 to turn OFF:1
    Press 1 to turn ON LED & 0 to turn OFF:0
    Press 1 to turn ON LED & 0 to turn OFF:2
fx >>
```

Serial Communication using MATLAB GUI

For exhibiting the Serial Communication utilizing MATLAB GUI, we will make two graphical catches utilizing MATLAB to kill on and the LED associated with the Arduino. Information will be sent sequentially from MATLAB to Arduino on tapping on these catches to kill on and the LED. Arduino will contain the code for getting sequential information from MATLAB and controlling the LED by sequential information got. Arduino code will stay same as past one, just contrast is that, beforehand we were sending sequential information '1' and '0' through direction window of MATLAB, and now similar information will be sent on ringing on two graphical catches.

To dispatch the GUI, type the underneath direction in the order window

guide

A popup window will open, at that point select new clear GUI as appeared in underneath picture,

Presently pick two pushbuttons for killing ON and the LED, as demonstrated as follows,

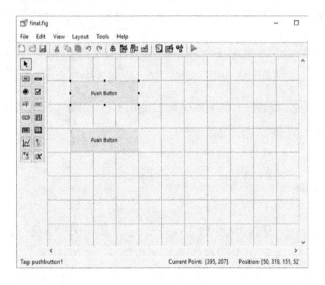

To resize or to change the state of the catches, simply click on it and you will most likely drag the edges of the catch. By double tapping on pushbutton you can change the shading, string and tag of that specific catch. We have modified two catches as appeared in underneath picture.

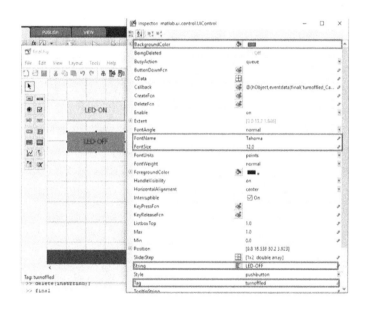

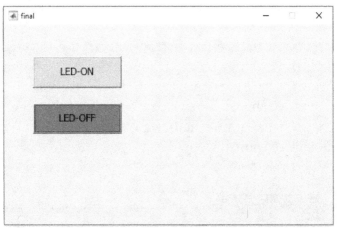

You can alter the catches according to your decision. Presently when you spare this, a code will create in the Editor window of MATLAB. Alter this code as indicated by the assignment you need to perform by your Arduino utilizing the MATLAB GUI. So underneath we have altered the MATLAB code. You can study Command window, editorial manager window and so forth in Getting started with MATLAB instructional exercise.

Complete MATLAB code, for building up Serial Communication among MATLAB and Arduino is given toward the part of the bargain. Further we are including the GUI document (.fig) and code file(.m) here for download (right click on connection at that point select 'Spare connection as...'), utilizing which you can redo the catches according to your prerequisite. The following are a few changes we accomplished for controlling the LED associated with Arduino.

Reorder the underneath code on line no. 74 to arrangement the sequential port and baud rate.

---

clear all;

global x;

x=serial('COM18','BAUD', 9600); % Make sure the baud rate and COM port is

% same as in Arduino IDE

fopen(x);

```
71
72      % Get default command line output from handles structure
73 -    varargout{1} = handles.output;
74 -    clear all;
75 -    global x;
76 -    x=serial('COM18','BAUD', 9600); % Make sure the baud rate and COM port is
77                          % same as in Arduino IDE
78 -    fopen(x);
79
80
```

where, fopen(x) is utilized to open the sequential port for sequential correspondence.

When you look down, you will view two capacities made for both the Buttons in the GUI. Presently compose the code in both the capacities as indicated by the undertaking you need to perform on snap.

In LED-ON catch's capacity, reorder the beneath code just before the arrangement to turn ON the LED. As you find in the underneath code, fprintf(x,1) is utilized for sending sequential information from MATLAB to Arduino sequential. Here we are sending '1' to the Arduino sequential and on the off chance that you check the Arduino code, you will find that Arduino will gleam the LED by making its thirteenth stick HIGH, when it gets '1' on its sequential port.

```
global x;

fprintf(x,1);
```

```
80
81      % --- Executes on button press in turnonled.
82    ⊟ function turnonled_Callback(hObject, eventdata, handles)
83    ⊟ % hObject    handle to turnonled (see GCBO)
84      % eventdata  reserved - to be defined in a future version of MATLAB
85      ⊢ % handles    structure with handles and user data (see GUIDATA)
86 -      global x;
87 -     ⌊ fprintf(x,1);
88
```

In LED-OFF catch's capacity, reorder the beneath code just before the part of the bargain to mood killer the LED. As you find in the beneath code, fprintf(x,0) is utilized for sending sequential information from MATLAB to Arduino sequential. In this part, we are sending '0' to the Arduino sequential and on the off chance that you check the Arduino code, you will find that Arduino will mood killer the LED by making its thirteenth stick LOW, when it gets '0' on its sequential port.

global x;

fprintf(x,0);

```
89
90      % --- Executes on button press in turnoffled.
91    □ function turnoffled_Callback(hObject, eventdata, handles)
92    □ % hObject    handle to turnoffled (see GCBO)
93      % eventdata  reserved - to be defined in a future version of MATLAB
94      % handles    structure with handles and user data (see GUIDATA)
95 -    global x;
96 -    fprintf(x,0);
97
```

In the wake of finishing with MATLAB GUI coding and arrangement the equipment as indicated by circuit chart, simply click on the run catch to run the altered code in .m record.

MATLAB may take few moments to react, don't tap on any GUI catch until MATLAB shows BUSY sign, which you can see at the left base corner of the screen as demonstrated as follows,

When everything is prepared, click on LED-ON and LED-OFF catch to kill ON and the LED. When you press LED-ON catch, thirteenth stick of Arduino goes HIGH and LED associated with this PIN starts shining, and when you press LED-OFF catch, thirteenth stick of Arduino goes LOW which makes the LED to mood killer.

Code

Arduino Code for Serial Communication between MATLAB and Arduino

```
int value;
void setup()
{
Serial.begin(9600);
pinMode(13, OUTPUT);
}
void loop()
{
 if(Serial.available()>0)
 {
  value=Serial.read();
  if (value == 1)
  {
  digitalWrite(13, HIGH);
```

```
}
if(value == 0)
{
digitalWrite(13, LOW);
}
}
}
```

MATLAB Code for Serial Communication using MAT-LAB GUI

```
function varargout = final(varargin)
gui_Singleton = 1;
gui_State = struct('gui_Name',    mfilename, ...
        'gui_Singleton', gui_Singleton, ...
        'gui_OpeningFcn', @final_OpeningFcn, ...
        'gui_OutputFcn', @final_OutputFcn, ...
        'gui_LayoutFcn', [] , ...
        'gui_Callback', []);
if nargin && ischar(varargin{1})
  gui_State.gui_Callback = str2func(varargin{1});
end
if nargout
    [varargout{1:nargout}] = gui_mainfcn(gui_State, varargin{:});
else
  gui_mainfcn(gui_State, varargin{:});
end
handles.output = hObject;
guidata(hObject, handles);
function    varargout    =    final_OutputFcn(hObject,
```

```
eventdata, handles)
varargout{1} = handles.output;
clear all;
global x;
x=serial('COM18','BAUD', 9600); % Make sure the
baud rate and COM port is
            % same as in Arduino IDE
fopen(x);
function turnonled_Callback(hObject, eventdata,
handles)
global x;
fprintf(x,1);
function turnoffled_Callback(hObject, eventdata,
handles)
global x;
fprintf(x,0);
```

10.STEPPER MOTOR CONTROL USING MATLAB AND ARDUINO

Stepper engines is a brushless DC engine that pivots in discrete advances, and are the best decision for some, exactness movement control applications. Additionally, stepper engines are useful for situating, speed control and applications which need high torque at low speed.

In past instructional exercises of MATLAB, we have disclosed that how to utilize MATLAB to control DC engine, Servo engine and Home machines. Today we will figure out how to control Stepper Motor utilizing MATALB and Arduino. In the event that you are new to MATLAB, at that point it is prescribe to begin with straightforward LED squint program with MAT-LAB.

Modes of operation in Stepper Motor

Before you start coding for stepper engine you ought to comprehend the working or turning idea of a stepper engine. Since the stator of the stepper mode is worked of various sets of curls, each loop pair can be energized in a wide range of strategies, this empowering the modes to be driven in a huge range of modes. Coming up next are the expansive groupings

Full Step Mode

In full advance excitation mode we can accomplish a full 360° revolution with least number of turns (steps). However, this prompts less dormancy and furthermore the turn won't be smooth. There are further two orders in Full Step Excitation, they are one Phase-on wave venturing and two stage on mode.

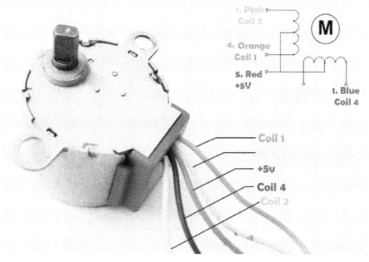

1. One stage on venturing or Wave Stepping: In this mode just a single terminal (stage) of the engine will be invigorated at some random time. This has less number of steps and consequently can accomplish a full 360° turn. Since the quantity of steps is less the current devoured by this technique is additionally low. The accompanying table demonstrates the wave venturing grouping for a 4 stage stepper engine

Step	Phase 1 (Blue)	Phase 2 (Pink)	Phase 3 (Yellow)	Phase 4 (Orange)

1	1	0	0	0
2	0	1	0	0
3	0	0	1	0
4	0	0	0	1

2. Two Phase-on venturing: As the name states in this technique two stages will be one. It has indistinguishable number of ventures from Wave venturing, yet since two curls are stimulated at a time it can give better torque and speed contrasted with the past technique. Albeit one drawback is that this strategy likewise devours more power.

Step	Phase 1 (Blue)	Phase 2 (Pink)	Phase 3 (Yellow)	Phase 4 (Orange)
1	1	1	0	0
2	0	1	1	0
3	0	0	1	1
4	1	0	0	1

Half Step Mode

The Half Step mode is the blend of one stage on and two-stage on modes. This blend will assist us with getting over the previously mentioned hindrance of the both the modes.

As you may have gotten it since we are joining both

the techniques we should perform 8-strides in this strategy to get a total revolution. The exchanging arrangement for a 4-stage stepper engine demonstrated as follows

Step	Phase 1 (Blue)	Phase 2 (Pink)	Phase 3 (Yellow)	Phase 4 (Orange)
1	1	0	0	0
2	1	1	0	0
3	0	1	0	0
4	0	1	1	0
5	0	0	1	1
6	0	0	0	1
7	1	0	0	1
8	1	0	0	0

Subsequently, it is your decision to program your stepper engine in any mode, however I lean toward Two Phase-on venturing Full Step Mode. Since this technique convey quicker speed then the one stage strategy and in contrast with half mode the coding part is less because of less number of ventures in two-stage strategy.

Get familiar with stepper engines and its modes here

Creating MATLAB Graphical User Interface for controlling Stepper Motor

At that point we need to construct GUI (Graphical User Interface) to control Stepper engine. To dispatch the GUI, type the underneath direction in the order window

> guide

A popup window will open, at that point select new clear GUI as appeared in underneath picture,

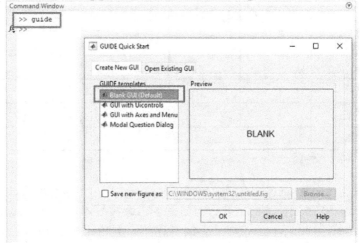

Presently pick two switch catches for pivoting the stepper Motor Clockwise and Anti-clockwise, as demonstrated as follows,

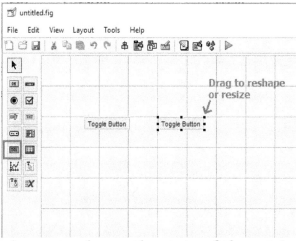

To resize or to change the state of the catch, simply click on it and you will probably drag the edges of the catch. By double tapping on switch catch you can change the shading, string and tag of that specific catch. We have altered two catches as appeared in beneath picture.

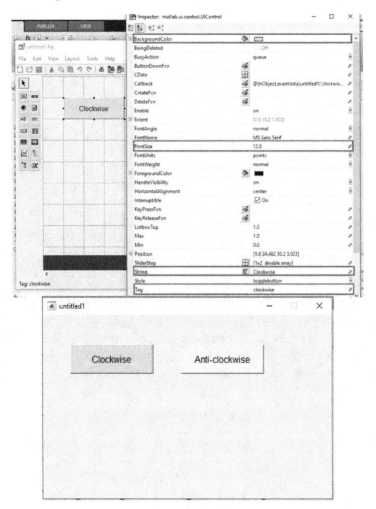

You can tweak the catches according to your decision. Presently when you spare this, a code is created in the Editor window of MATLAB. To code your Arduino for playing out any undertaking identified with your task, you generally need to alter this produced code. So underneath we have altered the MATLAB code. You can study Command window, supervisor window and so forth in Getting started with MATLAB instructional exercise.

MATLAB Code for controlling Stepper Motor with Arduino

Complete MATLAB code, for controlling Stepper engine, is given toward the part of the bargain. Further we are including the GUI record (.fig) and code file(.m) here for download (right click on connection at that point select 'Spare connection as...')), utilizing which you can redo the catches according to your necessity. The following are a few changes we accomplished for pivoting the Stepper Motor clockwise and anticlockwise utilizing two switch catches.

Reorder the underneath code on line no. 74 to ensure that the Arduino is chatting with MATLAB each time you run the m-record.

```
clear all;

global a;

a = arduino();
```

```
71
72        % Get default command line output from handles structure
73 -      varargout{1} = handles.output;
74 -      clear all;
75 -      global a;
76 -      a = arduino();
```

When you look down, you will view two capacities made for both the Buttons in the GUI. Presently compose the code in both the capacities as per the errand you need to perform on snap.

In Clockwise catch's capacity, reorder the beneath code just before the part of the bargain to pivot the engine clockwise way. For persistently turning the stepper engine clockwise way, we are utilizing while circle to rehash the two stage on venturing full mode ventures for clockwise course.

```
while get(hObject,'Value')

global a;

writeDigitalPin(a, 'D8', 1);

writeDigitalPin(a, 'D9', 0);

writeDigitalPin(a, 'D10', 0);

writeDigitalPin(a, 'D11', 1);

pause(0.0002);
```

```
writeDigitalPin(a, 'D8', 0);

writeDigitalPin(a, 'D9', 0);

writeDigitalPin(a, 'D10', 1);

writeDigitalPin(a, 'D11', 1);

pause(0.0002);

writeDigitalPin(a, 'D8', 0);

writeDigitalPin(a, 'D9', 1);

writeDigitalPin(a, 'D10', 1);

writeDigitalPin(a, 'D11', 0);

pause(0.0002);

writeDigitalPin(a, 'D8', 1);

writeDigitalPin(a, 'D9', 1);

writeDigitalPin(a, 'D10', 0);

writeDigitalPin(a, 'D11', 0);

pause(0.0002);
```

end

```
79     % --- Executes on button press in clockwise.
80     function clockwise_Callback(hObject, eventdata, handles)
81     % hObject    handle to clockwise (see GCBO)
82     % eventdata  reserved - to be defined in a future version of MATLAB
83     % handles    structure with handles and user data (see GUIDATA)
84
85     % Hint: get(hObject,'Value') returns toggle state of clockwise
86     while get(hObject,'Value')
87     global a;
88     writeDigitalPin(a, 'D8', 1);
89     writeDigitalPin(a, 'D9', 0);
90     writeDigitalPin(a, 'D10', 0);
91     writeDigitalPin(a, 'D11', 1);
92     pause(0.0002);
93     writeDigitalPin(a, 'D8', 0);
94     writeDigitalPin(a, 'D9', 0);
95     writeDigitalPin(a, 'D10', 1);
96     writeDigitalPin(a, 'D11', 1);
97     pause(0.0002);
98     writeDigitalPin(a, 'D8', 0);
99     writeDigitalPin(a, 'D9', 1);
100    writeDigitalPin(a, 'D10', 1);
101    writeDigitalPin(a, 'D11', 0);
102    pause(0.0002);
103    writeDigitalPin(a, 'D8', 1);
104    writeDigitalPin(a, 'D9', 1);
105    writeDigitalPin(a, 'D10', 0);
106    writeDigitalPin(a, 'D11', 0);
107    pause(0.0002);
108    end
```

Presently in Anti-clockwise catch's capacity, glue the underneath code at the of the capacity to turn the engine in against clockwise course. For consistently turning the stepper engine in against clockwise heading, we are utilizing while circle to rehash the two stage on venturing full mode ventures for hostile to clockwise bearing.

```
while get(hObject,'Value')

global a;

writeDigitalPin(a,'D8',1);

writeDigitalPin(a,'D9',1);

writeDigitalPin(a,'D10',0);

writeDigitalPin(a,'D11',0);

pause(0.0002);

writeDigitalPin(a,'D8',0);

writeDigitalPin(a,'D9',1);

writeDigitalPin(a,'D10',1);

writeDigitalPin(a,'D11',0);

pause(0.0002);

writeDigitalPin(a,'D8',0);

writeDigitalPin(a,'D9',0);
```

```
writeDigitalPin(a, 'D10', 1);

writeDigitalPin(a, 'D11', 1);

pause(0.0002);

writeDigitalPin(a, 'D8', 1);

writeDigitalPin(a, 'D9', 0);

writeDigitalPin(a, 'D10', 0);

writeDigitalPin(a, 'D11', 1);

pause(0.0002);

end
```

```
111    % --- Executes on button press in anticlockwise.
112  ⊟ function anticlockwise_Callback(hObject, eventdata, handles)
113  ⊟ % hObject     handle to anticlockwise (see GCBO)
114    % eventdata  reserved - to be defined in a future version of MATLAB
115    % handles    structure with handles and user data (see GUIDATA)
116
117    % Hint: get(hObject,'Value') returns toggle state of anticlockwise
118 -  ⊟ while get(hObject,'Value')
119 -     global a;
120 -     writeDigitalPin(a, 'D8', 1);
121 -     writeDigitalPin(a, 'D9', 1);
122 -     writeDigitalPin(a, 'D10', 0);
123 -     writeDigitalPin(a, 'D11', 0);
124 -     pause(0.0002);
125 -     writeDigitalPin(a, 'D8', 0);
126 -     writeDigitalPin(a, 'D9', 1);
127 -     writeDigitalPin(a, 'D10', 1);
128 -     writeDigitalPin(a, 'D11', 0);
129 -     pause(0.0002);
130 -     writeDigitalPin(a, 'D8', 0);
131 -     writeDigitalPin(a, 'D9', 0);
132 -     writeDigitalPin(a, 'D10', 1);
133 -     writeDigitalPin(a, 'D11', 1);
134 -     pause(0.0002);
135 -     writeDigitalPin(a, 'D8', 1);
136 -     writeDigitalPin(a, 'D9', 0);
137 -     writeDigitalPin(a, 'D10', 0);
138 -     writeDigitalPin(a, 'D11', 1);
139 -     pause(0.0002);
140 -  ⌐ end
```

Material Required

1. Arduino UNO

2. MATLAB introduced Laptop (Preference: R2016a or above forms)

3. ULN2003 - Stepper engine driver

4. Stepper Motor (28BYJ-48, 5VDC)

Circuit Diagram

Anbazhagan k

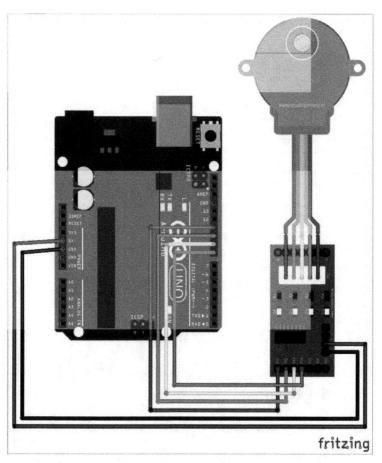

Controlling Stepper Motor with MATLAB

After arrangement the equipment as indicated by circuit chart, simply click on the run catch to run the altered code in .m document

MATLAB may take few moments to react, don't tap on any GUI catches until MATLAB is demonstrating occupied message in the lower side of left corner as demonstrated as follows,

When everything is prepared, click on clockwise or anticlockwise catch to pivot the engine. As we are utilizing switch catch, the stepper engine will constantly move clockwise way until we press the catch once more. Likewise, by squeezing the counter clockwise switch catch, engine starts turning in hostile to clockwise heading until we press the catch once more.

Code

```
function varargout = untitled1(varargin)
gui_Singleton = 1;
gui_State = struct('gui_Name',    mfilename, ...
        'gui_Singleton', gui_Singleton, ...
        'gui_OpeningFcn', @untitled1_OpeningFcn, ...
        'gui_OutputFcn', @untitled1_OutputFcn, ...
        'gui_LayoutFcn', [], ...
        'gui_Callback',  []);
if nargin && ischar(varargin{1})
  gui_State.gui_Callback = str2func(varargin{1});
end
if nargout
    [varargout{1:nargout}] = gui_mainfcn(gui_State, varargin{:});
else
  gui_mainfcn(gui_State, varargin{:});
end
function untitled1_OpeningFcn(hObject, eventdata,
```

```
handles, varargin)
function varargout = untitled1_OutputFcn(hObject,
eventdata, handles)
varargout{1} = handles.output;
clear all;
global a;
a = arduino();
function clockwise_Callback(hObject, eventdata,
handles)
while get(hObject,'Value')
global a;
writeDigitalPin(a, 'D8', 1);
writeDigitalPin(a, 'D9', 0);
writeDigitalPin(a, 'D10', 0);
writeDigitalPin(a, 'D11', 1);
pause(0.0002);
writeDigitalPin(a, 'D8', 0);
writeDigitalPin(a, 'D9', 0);
writeDigitalPin(a, 'D10', 1);
writeDigitalPin(a, 'D11', 1);
pause(0.0002);
writeDigitalPin(a, 'D8', 0);
writeDigitalPin(a, 'D9', 1);
writeDigitalPin(a, 'D10', 1);
writeDigitalPin(a, 'D11', 0);
pause(0.0002);
writeDigitalPin(a, 'D8', 1);
writeDigitalPin(a, 'D9', 1);
writeDigitalPin(a, 'D10', 0);
writeDigitalPin(a, 'D11', 0);
```

Anbazhagan k

```
pause(0.0002);
end
function anticlockwise_Callback(hObject, event-data, handles)
while get(hObject,'Value')
global a;
writeDigitalPin(a, 'D8', 1);
writeDigitalPin(a, 'D9', 1);
writeDigitalPin(a, 'D10', 0);
writeDigitalPin(a, 'D11', 0);
pause(0.0002);
writeDigitalPin(a, 'D8', 0);
writeDigitalPin(a, 'D9', 1);
writeDigitalPin(a, 'D10', 1);
writeDigitalPin(a, 'D11', 0);
pause(0.0002);
writeDigitalPin(a, 'D8', 0);
writeDigitalPin(a, 'D9', 0);
writeDigitalPin(a, 'D10', 1);
writeDigitalPin(a, 'D11', 1);
pause(0.0002);
writeDigitalPin(a, 'D8', 1);
writeDigitalPin(a, 'D9', 0);
writeDigitalPin(a, 'D10', 0);
writeDigitalPin(a, 'D11', 1);
pause(0.0002);
end
```

Thank you !!!